# WHAT TO DO WHEN YOUR FAITH IS CHALLENGED

# WHAT TO DO WHEN
# YOUR FAITH IS CHALLENGED

*by*
*Dr. Leroy Thompson Sr.*

**Harrison House**
Tulsa, Oklahoma

*What To Do When Your Faith Is Challenged*
ISBN 1-57794-188-8
Copyright © 1999 by Dr. Leroy Thompson Sr.
Ever Increasing Word Ministries
P. O. Box 7
Darrow, Louisiana 70725

Published by Harrison House, Inc.
P. O. Box 35035
Tulsa, Oklahoma 74153

# Contents

# Introduction

Although I have been a diligent student of the Word for many years, it was only recently that the Lord gave me one of the best lessons on faith that I'd ever received. He taught it to me through His Word and through experience.

I had my faith out really strong in a particular area, and at one point, it seemed as if everything started going wrong. I was tempted to have a pity party with just me, my flesh and my problem when, suddenly, the Lord spoke to me. He called me by name, and He asked me, "What would you do if you were fighting for your life? Would you just sit there, or would you fight? Well, you are not fighting for your life. You've got an outside problem, and you're not standing up to it."

Then I heard these words: "What to do when your faith is challenged."

That is how I received the message in this book. The challenge I faced was not so much against me as it was against God and His Word. The Lord taught me how to fight the good fight of faith so I could get the battle out of my hands and into His. Every step of the way, He led me and saw me through victoriously. He also taught me how to maintain my spiritual stand no matter how hot the "fire" gets, which is a prerequisite for having faith that wins.

Today, that challenge is just a memory. My faith is stronger, I am walking in more victory than I have ever walked in before and my God gets all the glory for what was accomplished.

The Lord has made it possible for us to have victory in every one of life's battles that we encounter. That means you have the supernatural ability to win over all the challenges to your faith that confront you! The tests and trials of life come to all of us at some time or another. It's what you do when the tests come that determines whether you will overcome.

I want to encourage you with this book *What To Do When Your Faith Is Challenged.* The information contained in these pages can help you face your test, withstand it and be gloriously delivered by the power of God!

# Chapter 1

## What It Means To Fight
## the Good Fight of Faith

*Fight the good fight of faith, lay hold on eternal life,*
*whereunto thou art also called, and hast professed*
*a good profession before many witnesses.*

—1 TIMOTHY 6:12

God calls the fight of faith a *"good* fight." The reason it is a good fight is that if you fight right, you will always win! In other words, if you fight the faith fight properly and stick with it, it will be a fight that you will win!

The apostle Paul didn't just say, "Fight the fight of faith." No, he said, "Fight the *good* fight of faith." Also, Paul didn't say, "Fight the *devil."* So many Christians are fighting the devil. They are fighting a defeated foe! Jesus defeated the devil in His death, burial and resurrection. So we don't have to fight the devil. We just have to know our position in Christ—that we are seated with Him in heavenly places (Ephesians 2:6). We also have to know how to wield the sword of the Spirit and to be led by the Holy Spirit, so we can *stand against* the devil.

You can be a Christian and be in Christ, but as long as you are here on this earth, Satan is going to try to get his hands on you. When he tries, that is when the wrestling match begins. But you are not to fight the devil; you are just to fight the good fight of faith. And if you fight properly according to God's Word, the devil will have to take his hands off you. I can prove that by the Bible.

**For whatsoever is born of God OVERCOMETH the world: and this is the victory that overcometh the world, even our FAITH.**

1 John 5:4

Now I want to submit to you that the word "whatsoever" means *who*soever. A "whatsoever" can't be born again, but a *who*soever can!

After reading this verse, can you see better why Paul said to **fight the good fight of faith** (1 Timothy 6:12)? Our *faith* is our *victory!* Our faith is our victory that overcomes the world, sin and Satan.

**We know that whosoever is born of God sinneth not; but he that is begotten of God keepeth himself, and that wicked one toucheth him not.**

1 John 5:18

Look at the first part of that verse: **We know that whosoever is born of God sinneth not....** That means he does not practice sin. Then look at the second part of that verse: **...but he that is begotten of God keepeth himself....** He that is born of God "keepeth" himself. In other words, he has a revelation of eternal life and knows that Jesus has already defeated the devil. He's *keeping* himself. The Bible says that when you do that, the wicked one "touches you not"!

How does the enemy try to get his hands on you? By trying to trick you into agreeing with him. He will use suggestions, ideas, pressures and circumstances to try to get you to believe his lies. They are only a bluff, but if the devil can get you to change your confession of God's Word to a confession of doubt, he can take the power of your own faith—what you believe—and use it against you. And once he gets you in agreement with him, he's got you!

10

## AGREE WITH GOD AND STAY IN VICTORY

The only way the devil can defeat you is if you agree with him. For example, if you're in strife, you're agreeing with the devil. If you get out from under the "umbrella" of grace, then you're agreeing with the devil. The enemy will use any number of avenues to get you off the right path. He will use trivial things of the flesh to try to get you riled up to the point that you're not walking in love. He will use symptoms and circumstances to try to get you to doubt God's Word and to agree with him that you're sick, defeated and going under.

When the devil tries to talk to you with his symptoms and lies, you need to rise up and tell him, "No, Mr. Devil, you're not going to touch me. As a matter of fact, you're not going to do *anything* to me. You are at the wrong house. I am redeemed. I am washed in the blood of the Lamb. I am healed by the stripes of Jesus. So get out of my house! Leave me and my family alone. I don't want to hear what you have to say."

You have to *resist* the devil—not *agree* with him!

**Submit yourselves therefore to God. Resist the devil, and he will flee from you.**

JAMES 4:7

Notice this verse is telling you something that *you* have to do. We have been trying to put all the responsibility on God. We've been saying, in effect, "God, *You* fight the good fight of faith *for* me." But, no, God told *us* to fight the good fight of faith.

## LEARN HOW TO KEEP *YOURSELF!*

Look at First John 5:18 again: **He that is begotten of God keepeth HIMSELF, and that wicked one toucheth him not.** This is where the

11

Church has gone wrong. People are trying to be "kept" by the pastor or some elder. But, no, you have to learn to keep *yourself.*

The enemy is a bully. He will try to put his hands on you. It's up to you to put the Word on him and stop him in his tracks. It's up to you to let him know that you are born of God and have eternal life. The pastor can only teach you so much—you need to study the Word for yourself.

The last part of First John 5:18 says, ...**and that wicked one toucheth him not.** That means that the devil's touch will never be a final touch on you. He will have to take his "touch" off of you if you are keeping yourself according to the Word!

The devil is no match for an informed believer who knows his rights in Christ. We don't have to fight the devil. He is already under our feet! Yet there are all kinds of warfare going on against the devil. Every time you look in some Christian magazines, you see something about spiritual warfare. But if a person just learned how to operate in *faith* and fight the good fight of *faith,* he wouldn't be having to wage so much "spiritual warfare," because he'd be keeping the enemy in his place. The devil's place is under our feet!

In First Timothy 6:12, Paul told us to fight the good fight of faith. He didn't tell us to fight the devil. He didn't even tell us to fight our neighbors.

I think some people misunderstood the Bible when they read that verse, and they began fussing and fighting with others! Sometimes people rub you the wrong way. Sometimes they treat you wrong. But you have to walk in the spirit of forgiveness. You have to walk in the spirit of love and continue to fight the good fight of faith.

Our text says, **Fight the good fight of faith, lay hold on eternal life, whereunto thou art also called, and hast professed a good profession before many witnesses.** The word "profess" in this verse actually means *to confess.*[1]

Really, by implication, a profession doesn't have as much power as a confession. Why do I say that? Because a lot of people *profess* to be Christians, and they are just professing. A lot of people *profess* that they have enough faith to move a mountain, but they are just professing. They have never moved a mountain of problems or circumstances in their entire lives.

### Confessing With Conviction

To me, confession is different. We who are saved have confessed Christ Jesus as Savior, and that kind of confession *with conviction* is the same pattern through which we confess other things pertaining to salvation, such as healing, material or financial blessings. Confession is God's system in which we believe something in our hearts and say it with our mouths.

Mark 11:23 is a classic example of believing and saying—of confessing with conviction.

> For verily I say unto you, That whosoever shall say unto this mountain, Be thou removed, and be thou cast into the sea; and shall not doubt in his heart, but shall believe that those things which he saith shall come to pass; he shall have whatsoever he saith.

This verse ought to inspire you to hold fast to your confession of faith without wavering, for God is faithful who promised (Hebrews 10:23)!

### Three "Twins"

The Bible constantly talks about confessing. And, as I said, the word "profess" in First Timothy 6:12 really means *to confess*. I want you to look at that verse again, because it is loaded with truths about how to receive from God.

FIGHT the GOOD FIGHT of faith, lay hold on eternal life, whereunto thou art also called, and hast PROFESSED a GOOD PROFESSION before many witnesses.

Do you see the three "twins" in this verse? The word "fight" is in there twice. The word "good" is in there twice. And the word "profess" (or *confess*) is also in there twice. They are three twin words that are in there to help you overcome when your faith is challenged.

## A GOOD FIGHT AND A GOOD CONFESSION

Let's look at the first phrase, **Fight the good fight of faith....** You know, some people in life are just fighting. They do not even know what they are supposed to be fighting! Other people are fighting a *poor* or *bad* fight of "faith." But, actually, if it's not a *good* fight, it's not really a *faith* fight!

As I said, a faith fight is a fight that you win! That's a *good* fight! Now, you are not going to win in life's fights just because you go to church. You're not even going to win just because you go to a good Bible-based, Word-preaching church! No, you've got to pay attention and apply yourself to spiritual truths. When you grasp the fact that you win in life's fights only when you fight them by *faith,* you will be well on your way to enjoying the victory that God meant for you to have.

Now look at another part of First Timothy 6:12: ...**and hast professed a good profession before many witnesses.** Paul is talking about confession, but then he goes on and talks about a certain *kind* of confession—a *good* confession. When you make a good confession, you know what you are talking about, and you are willing to stand by that confession no matter what happens. When you have that kind of attitude and that kind of confession, your confession will never let you down. Why? Because you're confessing the Word of God, and *God's Word* will never let you down!

14

Remember, your good confession must be backed up with a good fight—the good fight of faith. Just knowing something and saying it is not good enough. You must be able to stand on what you believe, or your confession alone will not survive.

So in First Timothy 6:12, Paul isn't talking about a regular fight; he's talking about a *good* fight. And he isn't talking about a regular confession; he's talking about a good confession. Say this out loud: "I am putting up a good fight, and I am confessing a *good* confession. And I will win!"

Now let's look at something else that's interesting about this verse.

**Fight the good fight of faith, lay hold on eternal life, whereunto thou art also called, and hast professed a good profession before many witnesses.**

**1 TIMOTHY 6:12**

Notice that in this one little verse, there are some present tense things for us to do now, and there are some past tense things that have already transpired. For example, the instruction to "fight the good fight of faith" is something for us to do now. Notice the next statement: "Lay hold on eternal life." That is another present tense thing for us to do now.

To "lay hold" means *to grasp.*[2] Paul is not talking about something we can physically grasp with our hands, but he is talking about laying hold on something we already have—our redemption in Christ—which not only includes salvation but also healing and freedom from poverty and lack. We do that by believing and confessing what God's Word says concerning our redemption.

Now look at the third statement: **...whereunto thou art also CALLED....** The word "called" is written in past tense. We have been called to eternal life and to this great redemption that God planned for us. The last statement in that verse says, **...and HAST PROFESSED a good profession before many witnesses.** The phrase "hast professed"

15

is talking about something in the past tense; it is something that has already happened. In other words, if you are saved, you have already confessed Jesus Christ as Savior. It's a past tense fact.

## THE DIVINE CONNECTION

Fighting the good fight of faith, laying hold on eternal life and confessing a good confession all have a divine connection. Understanding this divine connection will help you when your faith is challenged.

If you are a Christian, you have already confessed Jesus as Savior, and you became born again, a new creature in Christ (2 Corinthians 5:17). But once you enter that "door" of salvation, you have to *continue* to make certain good confessions in order to appropriate everything that belongs to you in Christ! You have to make good confessions—confessions with conviction—to receive your healing and to have your financial needs met.

In other words, if you are a Christian, your confession of Jesus as Savior in order to become saved is a past tense fact. It's a "done" deal; it's already happened. But after that, confession is still a continuous process. You must continue to confess the things you see in the Word that belong to you.

So, *first,* you were called. *Second,* you made a confession. First Timothy 6:12 talks about a *call* and a *confession.* But it also talks about a *fight.*

Fighting the good fight of faith will bring things into your life that you desire, and it will keep things *out of* your life that you *don't* desire! And if something comes against you that you don't want, such as sickness and disease, you can fight the good fight of faith to send it away from you. As I said, sometimes there is wrestling involved in this thing. That's why the Bible called it a *fight!*

16

You know, when you are in faith about something, you are not just guessing about it. You are like a bulldog "biting down" on what belongs to you in Christ. You don't care who tries to get you to turn loose; you hold firm, because Jesus has imparted to you eternal life and has told you in His Word about certain provisions that were made in the context of eternal life. So you lock your faith on those things. You say, "I'm not turning loose for the devil, demons, immediate kinfolks or my long-lost uncle from Timbuktu—I won't turn loose for *anybody!* I'm going to have what God says belongs to me. It's mine, and I have clamped my jaw of faith down on it! I am making a good confession, laying hold on eternal life. Healing, come into my body now. Prosperity, come into my life. Victory, you're mine!"

## LAYING HOLD ON ETERNAL LIFE

Notice again the part of First Timothy 6:12 that says, **Lay hold on eternal life....** Now some people think it's strange that in the same context Paul is telling us to fight the good fight of faith, he is also telling us to lay hold on eternal life. Someone might say, "Well, I've accepted Jesus. I thought I *had* eternal life." You *do* have eternal life, if you are a Christian.

Then, what does Paul mean when he talks about "laying hold on" eternal life? You received eternal life when you were born again. But when Paul says, "Lay hold on eternal life," he is telling Christians to *deliberately seek* eternal life. So he can't be talking about deliberately seeking to go to heaven, because Christians are already heaven-bound.

At a time when I didn't know any better, I thought that was what this verse meant. If you don't truly understand the revelation of this verse, you might think Paul is saying to Timothy, "This is what you need to do to lay hold on eternal life. Don't turn loose. Do everything right. Make sure you don't miss eternal life and go to hell."

But that is not what Paul is talking about. There are some things that are within eternal life which belong to us today that we should be receiving and walking in. In other words, because we have eternal life, there are certain provisions for us in this life. But they are things we are going to have to fight for—to *lay hold on*. They are things we are going to have to deliberately seek. We have to make it an aim of our life that we will not let ourselves be robbed of those things—that we are going to lay hold on them.

But how can you lay hold on what you don't know you're supposed to have? How will you know what to seek? There are many scriptural references to "seeking." The following are just a few.

> But SEEK ye first the kingdom of God, and his right-eousness; and all these things shall be added unto you.
>
> MATTHEW 6:33

> If ye then be risen with Christ, SEEK those things which are above, where Christ sitteth on the right hand of God.
>
> COLOSSIANS 3:1

> But without faith it is impossible to please him: for he that cometh to God must believe that he is, and that he is a rewarder of them that diligently SEEK him.
>
> HEBREWS 11:6

I like Colossians 3:1: **If ye then be risen with Christ, seek....** Paul is telling us to seek for something we already have. We are to deliberately seek to lay hold on eternal life. Once you do, and you realize that you have the divine life and nature of God inside you, you will double-dog dare the devil to tell you that you are down and defeated and can't get up! Why? Because you are risen with Christ. You are the head and not the tail, above only and not beneath (Deuteronomy 28:13). And Satan is under your feet!

As I said, for so long we have been trying to get to heaven. We have thought that heaven was all there was to salvation and eternal life. But remember what Jesus said in John 10:10: **The thief cometh not, but for to steal, and to kill, and to destroy: I am come that they might have life, and that they might have it more abundantly.**

## LIFE MORE ABUNDANTLY

When we say "life more abundantly," people automatically think about *things*—material possessions. Abundant life certainly includes *things,* but it's more than that. It includes the fruit of the spirit for example: love, joy, peace, longsuffering, gentleness, meekness, temperance, goodness and faith (Galatians 5:22-23). Walking in these characteristics will save you a lot of "headaches," arguments, pain and confusion in life. The fruit of the spirit is beyond the world's understanding. It falls within the scope, or grasp, of eternal, abundant life.

We talked about the *fruit* of the spirit—of the re-created human spirit. But also within the scope of abundant life are the *gifts* of the Spirit, the operations and manifestations of the Holy Spirit as He wills (1 Corinthians 12:6-11). The gifts of the Spirit consist of special faith, the working of miracles, gifts of healings, the word of wisdom, the word of knowledge, discerning of spirits, prophecy, divers kinds of tongues and interpretation of tongues (vv. 8-10).

So you see, abundant life includes all those provisions that were available for us through Christ—through His death, burial and resurrection—in God's great plan of redemption. When we accept Jesus, those things belong to us, but we are going to have to learn to fight the good fight of faith in order to possess them. We are going to have to lay hold on eternal life.

## WALK IN GOD'S FULLNESS THROUGH GOD'S WORD

Many believers don't realize the fullness of their salvation. They are beneficiaries, all right, but that does not mean that they're walking in all the benefits of their redemption. They aren't walking in the fullness of being the Father's sons or daughters. Just being a beneficiary does not guarantee that you're going to enjoy all the blessings of God. To enjoy the full benefits of eternal life, you have to know how to operate in *faith*.

I made up my mind a long time ago that I was going to learn how to operate in faith so I could walk in the full blessings of God. I took note of what Paul said in Second Timothy 2:15: **Study to shew thyself approved unto God, a workman that needeth not to be ashamed, rightly dividing the word of truth.** I found out that the Word of God will never leave you in a hole or at the bottom. Any "bottom" fights—fights of faith when you're at the very bottom—are always temporary when you're operating according to the Word of God. The Word of God is always alive, powerful and mighty, and there's always deliverance when you follow it!

The reason so many churches are doing nothing is that they're not teaching the Word of God. They're into psychology, man-made progress, humanism, social idealism and religious cliches. Most people will not drive very far for that kind of junk! No, you've got to give them the Word of God. If you give people the unadulterated Word of God, I don't care what town, city, hole or nook you're in, they will come for the Word!

I am a living witness of that. Our new church building is beautiful and spacious—and located on 100 acres in the middle of a cane field in a little place called Darrow, Louisiana! Darrow is about twenty miles south of Baton Rouge, and the church is about two streets away from the mighty Mississippi River. Darrow is such a small town that actually, some don't even call it a town. But we're preaching the Word, and people come to our church from all over the state.

Our text says, **Fight the good fight of faith, lay hold on eternal life...** (1 Timothy 6:12). Pay attention to those two statements. You've got to fight the good fight of faith if you want to lay hold on eternal life and the blessings of God that He has provided for us in His great plan of redemption. We already have the blessings; God has already given them to us. Most of us have been taught that. Now we just need to lay hold on them and appropriate them as ours personally. If we do not, we are going to be robbed.

As I already said, one benefit of eternal life is that we are going to heaven. But living successfully here in this world is another story altogether! There are other benefits of eternal life that provide for our needs today—in the "here and now." Those aspects are what God wants you to lay hold on. He wants you to know how to appropriate and put those things into practice every day of your life.

This is one of the confessions I continually make: "I have eternal life in me. Therefore, germs and harmful bacteria, you can't stay in my body. I have eternal life—the divine nature and power of God—in me. And the ability of God is in me to drive you out of me." That is one aspect of laying hold on eternal life. You have the Spirit of God on the inside of you, so you can say, "Greater is He that is in me than he that is in the world (1 John 4:4). Satan, whatever you bring, you have to take it back, because the greater One is living inside me now!"

## LAYING HOLD ON A LONG, FULL LIFE

Laying hold on eternal life will extend your life span on this earth. Psalm 91:16 says, **With long life will I satisfy him, and shew him my salvation.** The Spirit of God once said to me, "Tell the people I'll satisfy them with a long life if they will satisfy Me." Well, how do you satisfy God? Psalm 91:14 gives an answer: **Because he hath set his love upon me, therefore will I deliver him: I will set him on high, because he hath known my name.**

Another way to keep the Lord satisfied is to continue to fight the good fight of faith, laying hold on the eternal life that belongs to you. Also, you can keep the Lord satisfied by winning people into the Kingdom of God.

You see, that satisfaction which Psalm 91 talks about is a two-way street. Someone asked, "Well, what about prayer? Can't I keep the Lord satisfied with my prayer life?" Certainly, you must pray. You must keep up your prayer life. But the angels in heaven aren't rejoicing because you're keeping up your prayer life. They rejoice when someone is won into the Kingdom (Luke 15:10).

It's as though the Lord is saying, "There isn't any sense in My satisfying them with long life and leaving them on the earth if I can't use them and they just want to use Me."

So laying hold on eternal life is appropriating, activating and putting into practice what the Bible says about you and who the Bible says you are because you are born again—because you have eternal life. And one way you lay hold on it is through your confession. So begin to call out and confess the lifestyle you want to live—a lifestyle of walking in health and prosperity and of winning souls into the Kingdom of God. Say it out loud. Look into the mirror and say it. Say it in your car. Say it in your bedroom. Confess who you are. Say, "I have eternal life. I have the divine nature and ability of God in me. Thank God, I am going to live a long, satisfied life because I have eternal life in me now."

As the children of God, sons and daughters of God, we have special callings on our lives to do certain things in the Kingdom of God here on earth. But if we do not know how to fight the good fight of faith, that calling is null and void in the effect it's going to have on people or upon the situations of life.

Christians are called—they are called into the family of God, the Kingdom of God—and God has made available to them all kinds of advantages in life. He has given them the love of God shed abroad in their hearts by the Holy Spirit; the fruit of the re-created human spirit; the manifestations of the gifts of the Spirit; the sword of the Spirit, which is the Word of God; and the Name and the blood of Jesus. All of these things have been made available to those of us who are called; but if we don't know how to use them to fight the good fight of faith, the effect of our calling will be null and void. In other words, we won't be effective workers in the Kingdom of God.

When you believed in your heart and confessed with your mouth that Jesus Christ is Lord—when you accepted Him as your Savior, you made the "great confession." It is the great confession from which all other confessions for the things you need in life stem. But if you do not know how to fight the good fight of faith—how to stay in the faith fight until you win—your confession becomes null, void, powerless and of no use to you in this life.

## LEARN TO *PRACTICE* YOUR FAITH

One of the shortcomings of the Church is not so much the people, the money, the singing, the talent or the praise and worship. It's not even so much a shortage of the Word. It is a shortage of *action*, of putting into practice what we have heard. In many churches, believers have heard enough Word and enough teaching to turn the devil upside-down, inside out, and to just strip him naked, slap him "upside the head" and tell him to sit down and shut up! But not all of us have put what we've learned into practice. We get a revelation and say, *"Woo hoo!"* on Sunday; but by Wednesday, we are saying, *"Boo hoo,"* because life doesn't seem as though it's going our way. We have to hold on to that revelation and continue to work it until it manifests in our lives.

The Lord wants us to have a good life, and the good life does not consist of *things* or material possessions only. I've been around people with a lot of money, houses and cars, and some of them are just "hanging on"—they're not really living a good life.

In your own life, do you remember wanting something so badly and finally getting it? Maybe it was a new dress or a car or a house. You were so excited to get it, but after five or six weeks, the excitement wore off, and you thought, *So what. They're just things.*

So we know that *things* cannot really give us the good life. The good life lies in understanding your rights in Christ and knowing how to stand up against the adversary by fighting the good fight of faith when he comes against you. The good life is to be able to enjoy the Lord and His blessings, knowing that the devil can't touch your house, your life or your family. *That* is the good life! And God wants *you* to have it! He wants you to be prepared to fight the good fight of faith, to lay hold on eternal life and to win in *all* of life's challenges. This is the will of God for you!

# Chapter 2

## *Your Faith* Will *Be Challenged*

We know that we lay hold on the blessings and benefits of God by faith, and most of us understand the basic principles of faith. But what happens when you're operating in faith and, all of a sudden, your faith is challenged? The first thing you must know in fighting the good fight of faith is that *there is no such thing as unchallenged faith*. If you're living by God's kind of faith, your faith will be challenged. *This world* will challenge you. The *devil* will challenge you. *Situations* will challenge you. *People* will challenge you. Sometimes when people are challenging you, whispering and gossiping will go on about you. Rumors and lies will come out against you. Sometimes, you'll simply be persecuted because you are a child of God. That can be a challenge to your faith.

Your faith will be challenged in the form of the circumstances of life—stumbling blocks, hindrances and so forth. Things will come against you. There is not a utopian world you get to live in just because you are a believer. There will be challenges to your life even though you read the Bible, pray, live a holy life and praise and worship God.

You might say, "But I am a Christian; I have accepted Jesus Christ. I have been baptized in water. I am a member of so-and-so's church. I have my Bible and my notepad. I love God. *But I am still having challenges!"* We all do! As long as we are in this world, we are going to have challenges.

But overcoming challenges can become as simple to us as flicking off flies! You know when you start to swat a fly, it will take off. Well, challenges will respond to you that way if you learn how to operate in the Word of God properly.

Since we know that our faith will be challenged, we want to deal with those challenges effectively with the Word of God. We are children of God, and God wants us to meet the challenges of life that come against us. We meet those challenges by fighting the good fight of faith and by *continuing* in that faith fight.

Faith is an action; it is always moving. Faith is never stagnant. A simple definition of faith is *acting on the Word of God.* You see, if there were no challenges, there would be no need for faith or for acting on God's Word. We could just float through life, and everything would be easy. I mean, if we were living in some state of utopia, we would never have to believe God for anything. We could just be laid-back and never have to use our faith, because we'd know everything was always going to be hunky-dory. We'd never have any accidents. Sickness and disease could never touch our bodies. And money would always be in plentiful supply! We'd never have to read our Bibles, pray or go to church!

That may sound silly, but that's how ridiculous it is to believe that you don't need faith or that your faith will never be challenged.

## DON'T BE AFRAID OF FAITH CHALLENGES

A faith challenge occurs when you are believing God for something that is rightfully yours and the enemy comes along to challenge you, telling you that you can't have what you are believing

God for. And he will take it from you if you don't know how to face a challenge. The devil is a bully if you *let* him be a bully.

Just because we know that there will be challenges is no reason to become discouraged or disheartened. No, a thousand times, no! The Bible says, **For whatsoever is born of God overcometh the world: and this is the victory that OVERCOMETH the world, EVEN OUR FAITH** (1 John 5:4)! Challenges are nothing to be afraid of. I've had challenges in pastoring my church, but at the same time I have enjoyed myself! I've been having a good time! Why? Because each time I experience a challenge, it increases my stability and the capabilities of my faith.

So many people are afraid of challenges. They don't want any challenges to come their way. They want to just "roll over" and take it easy in life. But having no challenges is never going to happen in this life, so we might as well get ready for them. When we know how to face and deal with life's challenges, we will see God's goodness in ways we've never seen it before.

Sometimes when your faith is challenged, the enemy wants you to think, *What did I do wrong, Lord?* or *I'm living right. Why is this happening?* Don't pay the devil any attention. Just know that he is going to bring a "contest" against your life. He will contest your faith. The devil wants to see if you really believe what you say you believe. So, in order to deal with that "turkey," you just have to make sure you're really operating in faith! And you have to realize that your faith *will* be challenged.

If you can't accept that, you are a "cry-baby" Christian! God doesn't want you to be down and defeated. He says, **My people are destroyed for lack of knowledge** (Hosea 4:6). Refuse to be destroyed because of ignorance and a lack of knowledge. Learn to be ready for the challenges of life that come your way.

## WHY CERTAIN PEOPLE WILL BE USED
## TO CHALLENGE YOUR FAITH

Your faith *is* going to be challenged by the devil through circumstances or through people—even other Christians! I'll tell you why. The life of faith is a threat to many professing Christians. The life of faith is an inspiration to many sinners, but it is a threat to some Christians, for in the mirror of the life of faith, they see what they are supposed to be. That threatens Christians who are not living the life of faith. They become angry at those who *are* living the life of faith. After all, if no one were living the life of faith, then the failures of those who weren't living by faith could not be seen; we would all be just alike.

So you have to be ready and able to handle these challenges, because they are going to come. Some people are going to be threatened by your faith, and they're going to get mad at you. They are going to talk about you. If you don't learn to handle it, you will be worrying all the time.

Now, certainly, you are not *aiming* to be a threat to others. Your aim is to be a blessing. But there are those who will want to continue on the wrong path they are traveling, and when you decide to do what is right, you become a threat. Therefore, many times, they will lie about you and dig a pit, so to speak, for you. But the Bible says that he who digs a pit for another will fall into it himself (Psalms 7:15; 9:15; 57:6; Proverbs 26:27; 28:10; Ecclesiastes 10:8). So what are you going to do if someone digs a pit for you? You are going to just keep walking in love and trusting God.

People who lie about others had better watch those "gallows" they are building. Do you remember the story of Haman and Mordecai in the book of Esther? Esther had the king's favor, and she was able, through her position, to save her uncle Mordecai, whom Haman

28

wanted to kill. Haman had built gallows, hoping the king would order Mordecai's execution, but instead Haman ended up being hanged on his own gallows!

I wouldn't want to be "hanged" on the same lie I told about someone else. Would you? Those of us who are walking by faith in the fear of God would never lie about others, but these things happen every day. And it is really sad when Christians get into this kind of trouble because they don't follow the Bible.

### Satan Is the Accuser of the Brethren

You know, Satan is a liar and the father of lies, and he hates Christians. The Bible tells us in the book of Revelation that he is the accuser of the brethren (Revelation 12:10). But when someone accuses you, he's got to have someone to accuse you *to*. In one sense, the person who lies is not as bad as the person who "sucks it up"—who enjoys listening to those accusations! Then, when they find out one of their accusations is not true, all of their joy is gone because their joy was having something to "feed on"—something bad to think and talk about. Then, many times when they find out that it is not true, they act like they had never said or heard anything. They join back in with the person they were gossiping about. People are funny.

So your faith will be challenged, even by other Christians who don't want you to prosper and be happy in life. When you make up your mind to move up in the life of faith, you can expect your faith to be challenged. Heaviness can try to hang over your head if you are going to live the life of faith.

Why do I say that? I don't say it to discourage you, but if you can't handle hatred, envy, lies, rumors and false accusations, it would be wise for you to turn in your faith "credentials" and get out of the faith fight right now! You should just take your stand with those who live religious, traditional lifestyles. That way, you'd have a larger crowd going your way—more people who'd be on your side. You'd have less hatred and envy and fewer lies, rumors and false accusations. It is very easy to flow downstream with the currents flowing with you, not against you.

You know, faith and envy are enemies. "Envy" means *resentful awareness of another's advantage.*[1] When someone is envious, that means he is unhappy about your success and will try to do something to stop you. He wants you to fail. But if you want to live the life of faith, you have to be willing to go upstream, against the current of envy.

## UNFETTERED LIES AND UNGUARDED EARS

Do you know what a rumor is? I'll give you my definition. A rumor is a lie that has fallen on the unguarded ears of people who didn't have enough spiritual sense to keep what they heard to themselves! A rumor is a widespread statement with no truth to it. To start or spread a rumor means to disclose something, often of questionable truthfulness or accuracy, that is best kept to one's self. Rumors are common talk. Anyone can start or spread a rumor. It takes a person of faith who walks closely with God to stop a rumor in its tracks and refuse to listen to it or spread it around to others.

When I think of rumors, I often think of whispering. There used to be two nightclubs located right across the street from each other in a city near our church. One was called Rumors and the other was called Whispers. Those two things—rumors and whispers—should not be in the Church. Unfortunately, sometimes they are.

But if your faith is challenged through people—through rumors, whispers and accusations—don't worry about it. As long as there are people who will yield themselves to the flesh and the devil, those things will be here until Jesus comes. So don't worry. Just arm yourself with godly wisdom from the Word so you can stand against those challenges properly.

Now, Jesus told us in the book of Revelation that accusations would come against you. Jesus also said, "I was persecuted, and you will be persecuted" (John 15:20). The closer you get to walking like Jesus, the more opposition you are going to have. If you don't want the opposition, then stay mediocre. Just blend in with everybody else.

## GET OUT OF YOUR COMFORT ZONE
## AND FORGET TRYING TO PLEASE THE CROWD

Some Christians reach a certain level in their faith—we'll call it their "comfort zone." They don't want to go any further because they don't want to stir anybody's nest. They don't want to make anyone else angry or uncomfortable.

But, you see, faith is a progressive thing. You should go to higher heights every day in your faith. There are those who will try to call you down as you're climbing those heights. They'll say, "Stop. That's enough. I don't want to see anymore. I don't want to hear anymore." But don't listen to those voices. Keep climbing. Tell them, "You can come with me if you want to, but you can forget trying to call me back down. I'm not coming down."

## DON'T BE DISTRACTED FROM YOUR FAITH

I remember reading about Nehemiah and his people rebuilding the city wall. Enemies were making a mockery of God's people, and Nehemiah wanted to set the devil straight and get the city wall rebuilt. His enemy sent word to him and said he wanted to talk. Nehemiah said, "Why should I come down off the wall and let the work go undone while I am talking with you?" (Nehemiah 6:3).

31

Nehemiah stayed on the wall. Then after he would not come down to talk with them, they started a bunch of lies and rumors to try to scare him and challenge him to come off the wall. But Nehemiah kept building the wall.

When you are fighting the good fight of faith, do not entertain the thoughts of the enemy. Don't come down from your "wall"—whatever you are building with your faith—to argue with someone who does not know what is going on. The time you waste arguing and trying to explain to them what is right could be used to do something else. They don't really want to know the truth. They are just trying to pull *you* down to their level of mediocrity. You ought to know who should not bring you down from your wall. You just can't help some people, because they don't want to be helped.

Now, in Nehemiah's case, his enemies, Sanballat and Tobiah, were trying to bluff him to get him to grow weary and faint in his spirit so he would stop the rebuilding of the wall. But Nehemiah would not compromise his faith or his convictions.

> But it came to pass, that when Sanballat heard that we builded the wall, he was wroth, and took great indignation, and mocked the Jews. And he spake before his brethren and the army of Samaria, and said, What do these feeble Jews? will they fortify themselves? will they sacrifice? will they make an end in a day? will they revive the stones out of the heaps of the rubbish which are burned? Now Tobiah the Ammonite was by him, and he said, Even that which they build, if a fox go up, he shall even break down their stone wall.

> NEHEMIAH 4:4-6

Do you see how Nehemiah's enemies were mocking him? When you are operating in faith, you are going to be mocked too. But don't pay it any mind. That mocking is only temporary. If you continue fighting the good fight of faith, you are going to have the last "mock"!

You are going to make your mark, just as Nehemiah did, and it is going to be undeniable.

Let's continue reading in Nehemiah.

> **Hear, O our God; for we are despised: and turn their reproach upon their own head, and give them for a prey in the land of captivity: And cover not their iniquity, and let not their sin be blotted out from before thee: for they have provoked thee to anger before the builders. So built we the wall; and all the wall was joined together unto the half thereof: for the people had a mind to work.**
>
> NEHEMIAH 4:1-3

The people did not entertain the thoughts of the enemy. The enemy was trying to put fear in the hearts of the people. But verse 6 says, **All the wall was joined together unto the half thereof: for the people had a mind to work!** They kept their minds on their assignment—on the vision God had given them and on what He had told them to do.

God is not pleased when you let people or things hinder you from operating in faith. So when the lies, rumors and false accusations come against you, don't come down off your wall to answer all that junk! You'll just be wasting your time.

Now, if you get your little feelings hurt easily, you can't live by faith. If that is you, you need to get out of the faith business now, because there will be plenty of opportunities for your feelings to be hurt. Someone might say, "But I don't *want* to have my feelings hurt, Reverend Thompson." Well, it's better than getting your *faith* hurt!

## DON'T TRY TO DEAL WITH SPIRITUAL THINGS IN THE FLESH

Some people say, "I know what I'll do. I'll just deal with the lies, rumors and false accusations." But it's not often that you can deal with those things without starting a fight. You might say, "Yes, but I'm going to get this mess straight." You don't need to get it straight. It is already straight—it is a straight *lie!* You don't have to deal with it. Let the Lord deal with it. You just keep on building.

There are three more verses in Nehemiah 4 that I want you to see.

**But it came to pass, that when Sanballat, and Tobiah, and the Arabians, and the Ammonites, and the Ashdodites, heard that the walls of Jerusalem were made up, and that the breaches began to be stopped, then they were very wroth, And conspired all of them together to come and to fight against Jerusalem, and to hinder it. Nevertheless we made our prayer unto our God, and set a watch against them day and night, because of them.**

NEHEMIAH 4:7-9

Look closely at verse 9: **Nevertheless we made our prayer unto our God, and set a watch against them day and night, because of them.** In the Gospels, Jesus instructed us to watch and pray (Matthew 26:41; Mark 13:33). We need to "make prayer unto our God," but we need to watch too. Notice, Nehemiah set up a watch, day and night, against the enemy. And you, too, need to set up a watch when you are in a faith fight. You need to watch who you hang around. You need to watch what they are saying and get away from them if they are not walking by faith and doing and saying the things the Lord wants them to. If you do not watch and pray, you'll begin to compromise your faith, and the world and the devil will take off with your goods.

Now look at the sixth chapter of Nehemiah.

**Now it came to pass, when Sanballat, and Tobiah, and Geshem the Arabian, and the rest of our enemies, heard that I had builded the wall, and that there was no breach left therein; (though at that time I had not set up the doors upon the gates;) That Sanballat and Geshem sent unto me,**

saying, Come, let us meet together in some one of the villages in the plain of Ono. But they thought to do me mischief. And I sent messengers unto them, saying, I am doing a great work, so that I cannot come down: why should the work cease, whilst I leave it, and come down to you? Yet they sent unto me FOUR TIMES after this sort; and I answered them after the same manner.

NEHEMIAH 6:1-4

When you are dealing with something in faith, the enemy will send his emissaries to try to pull you off your "project." But do not come down from your wall. Do not stop the work to come down to his level. The devil cannot stop you. He may tell you that he can. He may threaten you to try to get you in fear. But do not stop the work. Notice in verse 4, Nehemiah says, **They** [Sanballat, Tobiah, and Gesham] **sent unto me four times after this sort; AND I ANSWERED THEM AFTER THE SAME MANNER.** In other words, Nehemiah never wavered from his position. Every time the enemy would come to try to distract him, he just said the same thing and continued working.

## THE ENEMY WON'T GIVE UP EASILY, SO DON'T *YOU* GIVE UP EASILY!

Don't think the enemy is going to give up trying to defeat you just because you resisted him one time. Look at Nehemiah 6:5-12:

Then sent Sanballat his servant unto me in like manner the FIFTH TIME with an open letter in his hand; Wherein was written, It is reported among the heathen, and Gashmu saith it, that thou and the Jews think to rebel: for which cause thou buildest the wall, that thou mayest be their king, according to these words. And thou hast also appointed prophets to preach of thee at Jerusalem, saying, There is a

35

king in Judah: and now shall it be reported to the king according to these words. Come now therefore, and let us take counsel together. Then I sent unto him, saying, There are no such things done as thou sayest, but thou feignest them out of thine own heart. For they all made us afraid, saying, Their hands shall be weakened from the work, that it be not done. Now therefore, O God, strengthen my hands. Afterward I came unto the house of Shemaiah the son of Delaiah the son of Mehetabeel, who was shut up; and he said, Let us meet together in the house of God, within the temple, and let us shut the doors of the temple: for they will come to slay thee; yea, in the night will they come to slay thee. And I said, Should such a man as I flee? and who is there, that, being as I am, would go into the temple to save his life? I will not go in. And, lo, I perceived that God had not sent him; but that he pronounced this prophecy against me: for Tobiah and Sanballat had hired him.

You see, the enemy will not give up easily. In the book of Nehemiah, we see that Nehemiah's enemies tried mocking, threats, intimidation, slander, lies and accusations. They tried to bluff him, but Nehemiah held his ground. He recognized the schemes of his enemies, but he would not budge an inch. And his wall was built! He won his fight of faith!

Now, let me say one more thing about living a life that is clean, holy, righteous and above reproach. In verses 6 and 7, Sanballat's servant spoke to Nehemiah about a letter he was going to deliver to the king. The servant spoke about what was in the letter, saying, It is reported among the heathen, and Gashmu saith it, that thou [Nehemiah] and the Jews think to rebel: for which cause thou buildest the wall, that thou mayest be their king, according to these words. And thou hast also appointed prophets to preach of thee at

Jerusalem, saying, **There is a king in Judah: and now shall it be reported to the king according to these words.**

You see, that letter was a lie, but Nehemiah was a righteous man, and he maintained his confidence in God despite the slander. He said to that servant, **There are no such things done as thou sayest, but thou feignest them out of thine own heart** (v. 8). In other words, Nehemiah said, "You're lying. I am not afraid of you." Then he prayed to God, saying, **For they all made us afraid, saying, Their hands shall be weakened from the work, that it be not done. Now therefore, O God, strengthen my hands** (v. 9).

When faced with challenges and opposition, Nehemiah was bold enough to maintain his position and continue to trust God. In much the same way, if you are living right and the enemy throws his bluff at you, you can stand there confidently and withstand him. You can keep pressing on in faith. But if you are not living right, boy, you are going under!

Certainly, we all make mistakes. When I talk about not living right, I am referring to *practicing* sin. If you are practicing sin or living in sin—not living right—then you are not going to stand fifteen minutes in the faith fight, because the devil's got your number.

Notice what Sanballat's servant said in verse 7: **And now shall it be reported to the king according to these words. Come now therefore, and let us take counsel together.** But Nehemiah still would not compromise. And neither should you. You can't take counsel with the devil, anyway! He doesn't want to take counsel with you; he wants to *destroy* you.

When you are flowing with the Holy Ghost, growing and prospering, the devil and the world's crew want to stop you! They will put up all kinds of roadblocks and obstacles to try to stop you, and if you don't know how to operate in faith, you are going to get weak the minute any little thing comes against you. You will say,

"What are we going to do now?" I'll tell you what to do. Just do what you have been doing! Live the life of faith. Live clean and holy, and grow in your faith and in your walk with God.

Don't ever believe that you can live the life of faith in the comfort zone. Those people who go to a certain level in their faith life and refuse to go any further are going to go with the flow of the world, where there will be no challenges (and no victory!).

But I'm going to go all the way with the Lord. How about you? We need to realize that we have an enemy who wants to defeat us and who will challenge our faith at every turn. But we are not ignorant of his devices and schemes. We are ready and well able to overcome!

## Chapter 3

### *How To Certify Your Faith!*

When your faith is challenged, be careful not to turn to your flesh. Pay attention to that statement, because you're going to need it down the road somewhere.

This area of turning to the flesh is where many Christians miss it. It's so easy to turn to your flesh when things are going wrong. It's easy to try to go some route besides prayer, faith and patient endurance to try to solve some problem or challenge.

Probably everyone has experienced the disappointment of turning to the flesh when his faith was challenged. Even if you are a Christian, you're still human. You are a spirit, you have a soul and you live in a body (1 Thessalonians 5:23). Your spirit is reborn and has the life and nature of God in it. But your soul and your body are not completely transformed yet, and you are going to face challenges in your soul and your body every day of your life. And so, at one time or another, no matter how sanctified you think you are and how marked up your Bible is, you have probably turned to your flesh when your faith was challenged!

You see, your flesh always thinks it has the "answer." Your flesh wants to settle everything today or tomorrow. It doesn't want to fight the good fight of faith. Your flesh wants to deal with the problem in a sensual way, or from the realm of sense knowledge—what you can see, hear, smell, taste and touch. And, many times, your flesh gets you into deeper trouble!

The Lord showed me something from the Scriptures about turning to your flesh when your faith is challenged.

**For we wrestle NOT against FLESH AND BLOOD, but against principalities, against powers, against the rulers of the darkness of this world, against spiritual wickedness in high places.**

EPHESIANS 6:12

Notice what Paul said here: **For we wrestle NOT against FLESH AND BLOOD.** We don't wrestle with flesh; so if your faith is challenged and you turn to your flesh for the answer, you're going to be greatly defeated!

## DON'T REACT TOO QUICKLY TO A CHALLENGE

One example of turning to the flesh when your faith is challenged is reacting too quickly—reacting in anxiety instead of responding in peace.

**Wherefore, my beloved brethren, let every man be swift to hear, slow to speak, slow to wrath.**

JAMES 1:19

This verse is telling us, among other things, not to be too quick to speak. We need to pause when we are challenged. That takes preparedness in the Spirit, not in the flesh. For example, in the natural, it's better to carefully take shelter when you realize that a storm is approaching than to frantically run for shelter after the storm has already hit. Even if you take shelter after the storm has hit, you still have to be calm about it, because if you are fretful and anxious, you could hurt yourself or someone else by reacting in panic.

The same is true spiritually. When the storms of life come to challenge your faith, we should already be in position. We should know what to do. If we don't, we'll panic and give place to the devil. We'll react in fear instead of calmly responding in faith. Isaiah 28:16 says, **He that believeth shall not make haste.**

## Uncertainty Will Rob You of Victory

Let me share another passage with you that illustrates the danger of turning to the flesh instead of waging the fight of faith.

**Know ye not that they which run in a race run all, but one receiveth the prize? So run, that ye may obtain. And every man that striveth for the mastery is temperate in all things. Now they do it to obtain a corruptible crown; but we an incorruptible. I therefore so run, not as uncertainly; so fight I, not as one that beateth the air: But I keep under my body, and bring it into subjection: lest that by any means, when I have preached to others, I myself should be a castaway.**

**1 Corinthians 9:24-27**

You cannot fight a faith fight in the flesh. The faith fight is not a flesh fight. Laying hold on eternal life is not even a probability with your flesh, even though your flesh receives certain benefits when your *spirit* lays hold on that life. You cannot grasp, lay hold on or deliberately seek eternal life with your flesh.

Look at First Corinthians 9:26: **I therefore so run, not as UNCERTAINLY; so fight I, not as one that beateth the air.** Fighting uncertainly is fighting in the flesh, and you will never obtain lasting victory that way. If you are uncertain about something, Satan will talk you out of it. For example, if you're sick and you're uncertain about healing in the Word, you can read and quote as many Scriptures as you want to, and you won't get healed. Satan knows how to quote the Bible, too, and he will quote certain Scriptures back to you to try to trick you.

41

He'll say, "Yeah, but what about this verse?" And because you're uncertain, you'll begin to doubt, and he'll rob you of your healing.

If you are believing God for your healing, get rid of the uncertainty by applying the Word of God to your heart and by sticking with the Word. If you are single and are standing your ground for a mate, get rid of all uncertainty. No matter what it is you want to receive from God, uncertainty will hold you back; it will roll you right back into doubt and unbelief and rob you of the blessings of God.

So many Christians are unsure of themselves. They are uncertain of who they really are in Christ and what they possess as a result of the eternal life they received through Him. They are "beating the air" with their fists, but never getting anywhere in their Christian walks. They're not rising to higher and higher levels of victory in their lives.

We are supposed to be reigning in life through Jesus Christ (Romans 5:17). The Bible says, **The Lord is my shepherd; I shall not want. He maketh me to lie down in green pastures: he leadeth me beside the still waters** (Psalms 23:1,2). So, what if something is still going wrong in the natural? The psalmist David was not talking about those still waters being there only when everything is going right. No, you can get a drink even when "all hell breaks loose"! That's why you need to learn to fight the good fight of faith *certainly.* (I'll talk more about that later in this chapter.) You can't fight in the flesh and expect to win.

## FAILURE TO KEEP YOUR FLESH IN CHECK WILL DEFEAT YOU

Now look again at verse 27 of the passage we read in First Corinthians 9: **But I keep under my body, and bring it into subjection: lest that by any means, when I have preached to others, I myself should be a castaway.**

42

I'm talking about not turning to the flesh when your faith is challenged. Looking to your flesh will render your faith ineffective and hinder the flow of the power of God in your life. That's why Paul said, **I keep under my body, and bring it into subjection.** So often, when we read that verse, we think of adultery, fornication, gluttony and other sins. But it involves more than that. Paul said, **I keep under my body.** In other words, he was saying, "I keep my flesh out of this thing I'm dealing with." Then he said, "I bring my body into subjection."

What does "subjection" mean? It means *control.* In other words, when your faith is challenged, you've got to bring your flesh under control. Why? Because if you don't, it will try to take over and lead the way. The flesh says, *"I'll fix this; I'll take care of it."* For example, you could be praying, and your flesh will say, "I'm tired of praying. Let's go straighten this thing out now." If you don't keep your flesh under—under control—it will get you into trouble. You will be fighting uncertainly, just "beating the air" (1 Corinthians 9:26).

So we know that one way Christians turn to the flesh when their faith is challenged is by reacting too quickly. They don't pause long enough for their spirits to rise up and allow them to respond in faith instead of in fear and anxiety. A *second* way people turn to the flesh is by fighting uncertainly—by being uncertain of their rights in Christ. They are beating the air with their fists, so to speak. They are not being effective with their faith.

—⧓— WRONG WORDS CAN DEFEAT YOU —⧓—

A *third* way Christians turn to the flesh is through the wrong words they speak.

**Let no corrupt communication proceed out of your mouth, but that which is good to the use of edifying, that it may minister grace unto the hearers.**

EPHESIANS 4:29

43

Just two chapters later, in Ephesians 6:17, it says, **Take the helmet of salvation, and the sword of the Spirit, which is the word of God.** How do you take up the sword of the Spirit, which is the Word of God? *With your mouth!* With the words that you speak!

But listen to me carefully. You cannot take up the sword of the Spirit with the flesh—by speaking words that are contrary to the Word of God. You can't speak doubt and unbelief or let your tongue be used for other corrupt communication and still be taking up the sword of the Spirit. In other words, you can't gossip about and backbite others one minute, and then turn around and take up the sword of the Spirit the next minute. It won't work.

The Bible says, **For he that will love life, and see good days, let him refrain his tongue from evil, and his lips that they speak no guile** (1 Peter 3:10). It also says, **For by thy words thou shalt be justified, and by thy words thou shalt be condemned** (Matthew 12:37). So don't speak "condemned" words. Don't use your words to fight in the flesh. Instead, use them to take the sword of the Spirit and fight the good fight of faith!

A *fourth* way Christians turn to the flesh is by trying to figure everything out for themselves. If you're turning to the flesh, you're always asking, "How's God going to turn this around? How in the world is He going to do this?" But you don't need to figure anything out when you're walking with God. Just do what He tells you to do, and you won't have to worry about anything.

---

## LOOKING TO YOUR FLESH WILL DISAPPOINT YOU

When dealing with the challenges that the enemy brings, it is dangerous to turn to your flesh. The devil deals in the mental realm, but he is a spiritual being. So if you turn to your flesh, you are trying to combat the spirit with the flesh, and that won't work. If you don't deal with the devil in the spiritual realm *with the Spirit of faith,* you are going to get whipped.

Have you ever turned to your flesh instead of to the Word of God for answers? Some people have turned to their flesh so many times; you'd think they would have caught on by now that it doesn't work. I've turned to my flesh in the past, and, oh, what a struggle I encountered when I did that! Instead of coming out of the hole, the hole got deeper. Instead of my mountain moving, the mountain ran me over!

You will never win by turning to the flesh. You will only be defeated and disappointed. The struggle only gets worse when you turn to the flesh, and, instead of rejoicing in the victory, you will be hurting again before long!

Many Christians do not know what it's like to fight the good fight of faith and to *keep on* fighting the faith fight when their faith is challenged. They never go on to lay hold on the blessing, because they are only charged up when there's a church meeting going on. They can only stand their ground when they are surrounded by a host of believers. They end up turning to the flesh and missing out on the blessings of God.

You have to build *yourself* up in the things of God. Then when your faith is challenged, you can be like a bulldog that doesn't turn loose! That's the way you have to be in order to lay hold on the things of God. You have to get ahold of the Word and refuse to let anything pull you from it. To do that, you have to learn to stand up, as an individual, in the Spirit. You can't depend on your flesh or on others to try to get you through a test or trial.

I train my congregation at Word of Life Christian Center not to depend on me. I try to feed them the Word of God and teach them so much that they don't even need me. I teach my people to learn to receive counsel from the Holy Ghost. I want them to learn to stand their ground for themselves and to fight their own battles. When you learn how to fight your own battles, those are battles that you are going to win!

Look at Second Corinthians 10 to further establish the fact that we are not to turn to the flesh when our faith is challenged.

> **For though we walk in the flesh, we do not war after the flesh: (For the weapons of our warfare are not carnal, but mighty through God to the pulling down of strong holds;) Casting down imaginations, and every high thing that exalteth itself against the knowledge of God, and bringing into captivity every thought to the obedience of Christ.**
>
> 2 CORINTHIANS 10:3-5

Notice the phrase in verse 3, **We do not war after the flesh.** Now, that does not mean that the faith fight involves fighting the devil. The faith fight is not fighting the devil, yet it is still a spiritual fight, and you still have to stand against him. It has been said that if the devil can hold you in the mental realm of human reasoning, he will whip you every time. But if you will hold him in the realm of the Spirit, fighting the good fight of faith, you will whip *him* every time!

Have you ever had a faith challenge? Maybe it was in your finances. Maybe it was in your body. Maybe it was in your family relationships. We will be challenged in life, friend. But if we stick with the Word of God and learn how to fight the good fight of faith by standing on God's Word, we will win every time!

## WE ARE *VICTORS*, NOT *VICTIMS*

I believe in winning! Do you? I found out in life that I wasn't a victim. I found out that, in Christ, I've been made a *victor,* not a *victim.* When I discovered that, I made up my mind that I was going to win in the situations of life!

46

I also made up my mind that no matter who I teach the Word of God to, I'm not going to teach him *down;* I'm going to teach him *up!* I came from a denominational background in which preachers just fussed and said nothing. They preached on sin all the time and told people how no good they were. But when I go to the pulpit on Sunday morning, I tell my people about the goodness of God. I tell them that He is the healer. I tell them that He wants to supply all of their needs.

Our church is completely debt-free. The people in our church are happy, free and highly integrated, with white and black people walking shoulder to shoulder. And we're down in the deep South! The devil is a liar. He wants to keep people defeated, fussing and fighting all the time. The only thing that's going to settle *any* problem, including a race problem, is the Word of God. When men and women are truly born again, skin color doesn't make any difference. We can all shout together about the goodness of God!

### Certify Your Faith and Release the Flow of God's Power in Your Life

We talked about the dangers of looking to the flesh when your faith is challenged. We read First Corinthians 9:26, which says, **I therefore so run, not as UNCERTAINLY; so fight I, not as one that beateth the air.** Fighting the faith fight in the flesh is the same as fighting uncertainly. Now we are going to learn how to fight *certainly.*

Let's keep reading in First Corinthians 9.

> **Know ye not that they which run in a race run all, but one receiveth the prize? So run, that ye may obtain. And every man that striveth for the mastery is temperate in all things. Now they do it to obtain a corruptible crown; but**

we an incorruptible. I therefore so run, not as uncertainly; so fight I, not as one that beateth the air.

1 Corinthians 9:24-26

Look at verse 26 of this passage. Paul said, I...run, not as uncertainly.... You see, if you're going to fight the fight of faith, you'd better be certain about what you're doing. There are some who are running uncertainly, and as soon as a little pressure comes—some situation or circumstance that tells them they're not moving in the direction they want to go—they will go under. Why? Because they are running uncertainly.

The apostle Paul said, I therefore so run, not as uncertainly.... Therefore, he was running *certainly*. He was running his course, fighting the good fight of faith and laying hold on the promises of God. He wasn't turning to his flesh or depending on someone else to get him through.

One of the things you're going to have to do so you won't turn to your flesh is to *certify your faith*. I was preaching this message one time, and I heard the Spirit of God say, "You must certify your faith. You must *confirm* your faith." Your faith should have a confirmation.

Now let's look at that phrase "certify your faith." What does God mean by that? One definition of "certify" is *to testify usually formally and in writing to the truth or genuineness of something*.[1] So you need to certify your faith. Certify your faith and confirm it with the Word of God. If your faith is confirmed with the Word of God, then come "hell or high water," so to speak, you will stand your ground! If the devil came with a legion of devils, you would still stand your ground, look the devil in the eye and tell him to bow in the Name of Jesus! And he would have to obey you!

When you've got the Word of God hidden on the inside of you and that Word is working mightily in you, you're not afraid of the devil. You're not afraid of his cohorts. You're not afraid of devils, demons, sickness, disease, poverty or *anything!* You're not afraid of the reports that come via the news media, the doctors or the economists, because you have inside information. You know that you know, bless God, that you've already won! You're a winner, a victor, not a victim.

It's pretty good to start a race off at the starting line, knowing that you're going to win, isn't it? It's pretty good to know at the beginning how that race is going to end! Well, in the fight of faith, you could have demons at the starting line with you, trying to defeat you. They're wondering how it's going to end—who's going to get to the finish line first. You might have demons on one side and the devil on the other side, and you could still boldly say, "You think you're going to beat me? Don't you know who's going to win here? I've already won!"

You need to certify your faith. If the doctors say, "There's nothing we can do," where is your faith? Is it in the doctors? Is it in your flesh? Or is it in the Word of God? You must stand on the Word of God and certify your faith. Always let God have the last word in your life—in your battles—and He'll always bring you out in victory! *Always.* Remember, Paul called it "the *good* fight" (1 Timothy 6:12). It's a good fight, because if you are fighting it properly with the Word of God, it's a fight that you will win!

The good fight of faith is not simply a fight that you win. It's more than that, because there's something that *you* have to do—a part that *you* play. You have to stay in the fight! The good fight of faith is a fight that you stay in until you win! You don't quit. You don't stay wound up and pumped up for two or three weeks and then decide to give up. You don't stand your ground one day and go around complaining and murmuring the next. No, you have to certify your faith.

The Lord says, "Heaven and earth will pass away, but My words will never pass away" (Matthew 24:35; Mark 13:31; Luke 21:33). You have to make up your mind that the Bible is true and that the just shall live by faith (Habakkuk 2:4; Romans 1:17; Galatians 3:11; Hebrews 10:38). You have to make up your mind that faith is a lifestyle. It's not a temporary thing. It's not just a special meeting anointing! You've got to decide, "I'm going to have this anointing with me all the days of my life!"

### GOD IS NOT AN UNCERTAIN GOD!

Refuse to walk with uncertainty. God is not an uncertain god. He knows what He wants to do. He knows that He's brought deliverance to us through Jesus Christ. God knows that the Name of Jesus can change any situation. He knows that the blood has already delivered us from sickness, poverty and the curse of the law. God knows that He has given us the victory.

I found this truth out years ago, thanks to the Holy Spirit and some great men of God who preached the uncompromised truth of the Word. One ministry I have followed for years is the ministry of Rev. Kenneth E. Hagin, because God told me to follow him. Just in the last couple of years, I thought I was already following him as closely as I could, but the Spirit of God told me to follow him even more closely. I began to get ahold of every one of his materials and listen to his tapes and read and reread his books. God said, "I want you to stick with him. Follow him everywhere he goes. Wherever he is ministering, get on the plane and go." And my wife, Carolyn, and I have set out to do that.

I remember back in 1983, Carolyn and I were visiting Rev. John Osteen's church in Houston, Texas. We were just getting ahold of this message of faith. In that church, we saw all the people with their hands raised, praising and glorifying God. We were not used to that, so we just stood and watched, amazed.

Brother Hagin was ministering that day for Brother Osteen. I didn't know Brother Hagin from the next minister, but as I sat there listening to him, something profound happened to me. We were sitting off to one side of the auditorium, and I said, "God, I've really just gotten in the Word, and I want to hear what this man has to say. Would you bring him over on our side of the platform so I can see him better?" Right after that, Brother Hagin walked over and faced our side of the auditorium for the remainder of his message.

Now, as I said, I didn't know Brother Hagin at that time. If I had known him, I would have been even more humbled by what happened next in that meeting (even now when I tell this, I tell it reverently). With God as my witness, as I sat there watching Brother Hagin, the Spirit of the Lord spoke to me and said, "I have given you the same anointing." When He said that to me, a sense of humility came over me, and I got on the floor and began to cry and bawl. I even crawled around a bit, trying to get under a chair! My wife did her best to get me up and put me back in my chair (but if I had known who Brother Hagin was, I *would* have gotten under that chair!).

That's why I follow Brother Hagin's ministry so closely, and nobody is going to turn me around. I'm following "all the way" with that ministry because it's founded on the Word of God. And I'm going to support his ministry.

You can't let anything distract you from doing what God has told you to do and from fighting certainly, or certifying your faith. Sometimes, you need to think for yourself and not let anybody else think for you. I don't know what you're going to do; but wherever the Word rolls, that's where I'm going to roll! I'm sticking with the Word. I'm going to follow God and His Word.

Remember Paul said, **I therefore so run, not as uncertainly; so fight I, not as one that beateth the air** (1 Corinthians 9:26). Now look at the last part of that verse: ...NOT **as one that beateth the air**. My brother and sister, if you try to fight the faith fight in the flesh, you are going to be beating the air. What does beating the air do? It accomplishes nothing,

51

except to wear you out! You need to be walking by faith and fighting the good fight of faith instead of turning to the flesh.

## THE ROLE OF CONFESSION IN THE FAITH FIGHT

Many times, we are just beating the air, even in our positive confessions. We are confessing the Word, all right. But we are saying things we don't really believe. We're just talking.

You know, sometimes there's a time to confess the Word to change circumstances, and sometimes there's a time to confess the Word to change *you*. Sometimes you need to confess the Word to yourself to build it into your spirit so that it becomes real to you. *Then* you can fight certainly, not beating the air.

Also, did you know that there's a time not to confess the Word, but just to stand there with only thanksgiving and praise coming out of your mouth? After you've already believed and confessed awhile, sometimes you just need to praise the Lord because you believe that what you've confessed is true and that it is coming to pass!

So don't beat the air. So many Christians are beating the air about their finances, their health and their family relationships. They're trying to solve their problems through the flesh. But the Bible does not say, "We walk by sight, not by faith." It says, **We walk by *faith*, not by sight** (2 Corinthians 5:7). So if you're fighting the good fight of faith, and it looks like something is not going your way, don't worry about how it looks in the natural. Think only, *What is God saying about it?* Just trust God and obey Him.

## THE ROLE OF OBEDIENCE IN THE FAITH FIGHT

You might say in a test or trial, "Well, what am I going to do?" You already know what to do. The Bible said in Isaiah 1:19, **If ye be**

**willing and obedient, ye shall eat the good of the land**. Obey God. Be willing, and you'll eat the good of the land.

Are you eating the good of the land? Well, if you're not, you can start right now getting yourself in position by being willing and obedient to God no matter what anybody else says or does. If you trust God and obey Him, He will always back you up and make your enemies—the devil and demons—bow down. That's why *you* don't have to fight them. Jesus has already defeated them. You just have to certify your faith, stand your ground and fight the good fight of faith! God will take care of the rest!

# Chapter 4

## Learn To Rest in God's Timing

By way of review, we said that, *first,* in order to walk in the blessings of God, we must learn to fight the good fight of faith. *Second,* we need to realize that our faith *will* be challenged. *Third,* when our faith is challenged, we can't turn to the flesh and expect to receive the blessings of God; we have to certify our faith and stand strong on the Word, trusting God and obeying Him. And, *fourth,* we have to realize that God does not deal in the realm of time.

You see, when you're fighting the faith fight and you're dealing with a certain faith project, your mind may be on how long you've been standing your ground. But God does not deal with time; He deals with *timing.* If you don't understand the difference between the two, you can get into trouble trying to get your prayers answered on your watch, your clock or your calendar. If you do that, you'll mess up your faith fight.

There is a difference between time and timing. God is an eternal God. He is not on a twenty-four hour day like we are. But there is a certain timing in which God knows a particular thing needs to be carried out.

If you continue to be faithful and steadfast, your timing will come. And God is faithful. He is your Father. Don't think He is going to let the devil or anybody else put too great of a burden on you if you are believing Him. He is not going to put up with it. Would you let somebody put too much burden on your own child? No, of course you wouldn't. So why would the heavenly Father be any different? When you are trusting the Father, and He gets enough of your being burdened, He says, "Wait! That is enough! I'm going to get my child out of that problem!"

God is not just my friend; He's my Father. I am in the family of God, and He is concerned about me. But I need faith so He can move on my behalf. And my faith needs to be able to stand the test of time.

###### ➰ DIVINE DELAY OR DEVILISH DISAPPOINTMENT? ➰

God's timing is always right. *Sometimes, there are some divinely permitted delays in the manifestation of what you're believing God for.* In other words, sometimes God permits a delay. If you are fighting the good fight of faith—certifying and confirming your faith with the Word of God and standing firm upon it—and there is a delay, that is not the time to let go of your faith and give up!

You must not let Satan take God's divinely permitted delay and turn it into a devilish disappointment! You need to hold fast and learn to work with God. Sometimes God divinely permits things not to come to pass until He can get you in a certain position. But if you are operating in the sense realm, Satan will come along and tell you that your faith is not working. God may have more things that He wants to do for you, but if you yield to the devil and his lies instead of to God, the devil will take those very things God wants to do for you and turn the situation into a disappointment.

We all have experienced this at one time or another. We stood and stood in faith, and we were confessing the Word, but it seemed like nothing was happening. Then Satan came along and tried to bring up doubt, fear or some type of condemnation for something that was already repented of and under the blood of Jesus. When he did, we let go of our faith. We turned loose and missed the blessing. But, thank God for mercy and grace. If we are doing all we know to do, feeding on the Word and seeking God, then we have another promise.

**For if our heart condemn us, God is greater than our heart, and knoweth all things. Beloved, if our heart condemn us not, then have we confidence toward God.**

1 JOHN 3:20,21

God is bigger than our hearts. If the intents of our hearts are right, He can bless us. So don't let the devil condemn you. Maybe you did miss it somewhere along the way. Just repent and accept God's forgiveness. Maybe your faith was challenged, and you let something slip out of your mouth that you didn't want to come out. You didn't mean it, but you said it anyway. Just repent and confess it to God. Don't wait. Don't let those words hang around long enough to get in your heart. Don't meditate on what you said; don't dwell on it.

You see, Satan will always try to dig up something in your life that's already under the blood in order to try to hinder your faith. He'll say, "Remember this? Remember that?" When he does that, all you need to say is, "Satan, that's under the blood. I believe God. I'm not moved by what I see. I'm not moved by what I feel. I'm only moved by what I believe, and I believe the Word of God. I believe God said what He meant, and I believe God meant what He said."

The devil is the master of deceit and discouragement. He will try to discourage you when you are believing God. He will try to deceive you into thinking that your faith is not working or that God is not going to come through for you. For example, in the case of a single woman believing God for a godly husband, the devil will try to discourage her and trick her into running off with the next man who comes along. He will tell her, "You're a fool not to take this opportunity." Her heart might be telling her that the man is not right for her—that God has someone better for her—but she goes with him anyway and ends up sorry she ever met him. Little does she know that within just a short period of time, the right man would have shown up in her life.

As I said, the devil is the master of deceit and discouragement. And when he gets someone to fall for his lies, he becomes the master of *disappointment* too. Have you ever been disappointed in life? I have. Most of the time, I have been disappointed in myself. But, I tell you, God is not in the disappointing business! So don't let the devil turn those divine delays into something else. Learn to stand against him with the truth of God's Word.

> **For though we walk in the flesh, we do not war after the flesh: (For the weapons of our warfare are not carnal, but mighty through God to the pulling down of strong holds;) Casting down imaginations, and every high thing that exalteth itself against the knowledge of God, and bringing into captivity every thought to the obedience of Christ; And having in a readiness to revenge all disobedience, when your obedience is fulfilled.**
>
> 2 CORINTHIANS 10:3-6

God has told us in His Word how to stand against the devil and to wage a good warfare in the Spirit, fighting the good fight of faith. What did He tell us to do? To cast down devilish reasonings, imaginations and everything that exalts itself against God's Word. We've got to bring into captivity **every thought to the obedience of Christ** (v. 5).

I tell you, when you are walking by faith and fighting the good fight of faith, the devil wants you off the job! So you've got to keep your eyes on the Word and your face set like flint! That means you are not going to turn. You're not paying attention to what the devil or anybody else is saying, because you refuse to be pulled away from your faith.

However, you may be believing God for something, and He is divinely permitting it to be delayed to get some other things together for you. When your answer shows up, the delay will actually mean better dividends for you!

What will you do during a divine delay? Will you continue to trust the Lord? Proverbs 3:5 and 6 say, **Trust in the Lord with all thine heart; and lean not unto thine own understanding. In all thy ways acknowledge him, and he shall direct thy paths.** So just keep on working the Word during divine delays. Know that the Lord is adding on to what you are believing Him for so that you can have more than you asked for when He finishes with you! Stay on the line. Trust and be confident in the Lord.

## THERE IS NO SUCH THING AS A CHALLENGE TO GOD

Your faith is going to be challenged in life, but did you know that there is no such thing as a challenge to God? With God, it's never a challenge. You could name the biggest name you could think of in this world who might try to challenge God. But God can't be challenged. You could call the name of the biggest company or organization in the world that might try to stand up to God and challenge Him. But can anyone present a real challenge to God? No! Then, since there is no such thing as a challenge to God, if we stick with Him, how can *we* be defeated or left out?

Get ahold of the fact that there is no challenge to God. It is only timing with Him. Understanding that fact will help you stay in the faith fight until you see the answer. So just learn to stay steady in the midst of a faith challenge.

Now, when you are challenged and another person's will is involved, the situation may take a little longer. If you were just standing for something for yourself, you might get it right away every time. But you can't impose your will on anybody else. If you could, Jesus would make everybody get saved today. But, as you know, people are rejecting Him every day.

Has the devil ever tried to hinder you in your faith fight? If you've never been talked to by the devil, you've probably never fought the good fight of faith. You've never been a threat to his kingdom, because you're not doing anything. That's why he's not talking to you or trying to mess with you.

But once you start tearing the devil's kingdom down, he'll start talking to you. That's why you need to learn how to certify your faith and constantly confirm it by meditating on it and confessing it.

## REFUSE TO BECOME WEARY IN YOUR FAITH FIGHT

Let's look at some references in the Word to God's timing—to His divinely permitted delays.

**And let us not be weary in well doing: for in DUE SEASON we shall reap, if we faint not.**

**GALATIANS 6:9**

I want you to underline in your Bible those two words "due season." What are you believing God for today? Don't become weary about it. Continue to believe and act on what you believe, making the right kind of confession continually, and it will come to pass in due season. If you stick with the Word of God, God's Word will stick with you, and you'll reap what you've been believing Him for!

Now look at that phrase **And let us not be weary in well doing....** What is "well doing"? We're doing well when we're confessing the Word of God and we're trusting Him. We're doing well when we're living sanctified, holy lives and have our bodies under subjection. We're doing well when we do not fornicate, commit adultery, lie or steal. We're doing well when we refuse to go outside of God's system of righteousness. You know, God almost *has* to bless that! He has told us how to live, and He will "lock Himself into" somebody who's walking with Him.

## ARE YOU READY FOR YOUR ANSWER?

God *wants* to bless you. God doesn't want you looking across the fence at another man's pasture. God wants to give you your own pasture! The Bible says, **He maketh me to lie down in green pastures: he leadeth me beside the still waters** (Psalm 23:2). He's talking about *all* of His children, not just a few. But He's got to know He can trust you with it. If you get some of the things you're asking God for but you're not ready for them, your faith may be shipwrecked (1 Timothy 1:19).

Many times it's not the devil holding things back from you. You could be holding them back *yourself*. For example, if God permitted you to have a nice, plush home and a nice boat, where would you be on Sunday mornings? Would you be in church, or would you be propped up, taking it easy in your fancy home or out fishing in your new boat? Or, if God gave you a job promotion and began speaking to you about giving some of that money He'd given you to one of His projects, would you give it, or would you hoard it up for yourself? God doesn't want you to get so busy with your house, your boat and your money that you're not hearing Him like you should.

On the other hand, when God knows you're going to hear Him and support Kingdom business and the spreading of the Gospel, you can get ready for promotion, because Psalm 75:6-7 says that promotion comes from the Lord. God has promoted some people who have turned around and held back on Him. They need to go ahead and turn loose of some of that money that He's talking to them about. It's the only way they're going to continue to be blessed.

Let's look again at Galatians 6:9: **And let us not be weary in well doing: for in due season we shall reap, if we faint not.** Now Paul didn't say we *might* reap in the "sweet by and by" when it's all over down here. No, he said, **We *shall* reap *if* we faint not!** Paul qualified the blessing by saying, "if we faint not." According to *The Amplified Bible*, to "faint" means *to lose heart; to give up; to quit; or to cave in.* If we don't lose heart, give up, quit or cave in, then in due season, we'll reap.

## GOD'S TIMING IN THE MATTER OF A MATE

Now remember, I said that God does not deal with time. I like to teach this in reference to single women, to minister to them and put them at rest. Many of them are waiting to meet their mates. But if you're a single woman who's walking with God, just walk clean. Walk holy and live for God. He has your mate. Believe Him for your husband. Don't try to rush it, because when you rush it, you will be looking to the flesh. Then you will end up with somebody whom God did not send, and you will have problems all the rest of your life as a result. So just wait on God. Just be pretty for God. Love Him and wait before Him. Hold fast to your confession of faith without wavering, for He is faithful that promised (Hebrews 10:23).

I've seen so many single ladies concerned about their age and the time that's passing. Don't worry about the time. Enjoy God every day. Get involved in Kingdom business and serve Him. He will take care of it. He is working on it for you.

There is a due season with God. You may be believing God for a certain thing right now. Whether it be a mate, healing, finances or something else, just stick with it. Stay with your believing, and hold fast to your confession of faith. God is faithful, and He never loses!

## YOU MUST BEGIN AND FINISH IN FAITH

Romans 1:17 talks about going "from faith to faith":

**For therein is the righteousness of God revealed from faith to faith: as it is written, The just shall live by faith.**

Notice that verse *doesn't* say, "from faith to *love*." Certainly, you have to walk in love. Faith works by love (Galatians 5:6). But, you see, when you start a faith project, *at the beginning, in between* and *at the end,* you must be in faith. You must *begin* in faith and *finish* in faith. And the way to do that is to look to Jesus, the author and finisher of our faith.

**Looking unto Jesus the author and finisher of our faith; who for the joy that was set before him endured the cross, despising the shame, and is set down at the right hand of the throne of God.**

**HEBREWS 12:2**

Notice, Jesus is the "author." What does that mean? It means your faith originated with Him. And not only is He the author, He is the finisher too. So, you see, that's why Romans 1:17 says, **from faith to faith.** We are to begin and finish in faith. We are to start in faith and stand in faith until that which we are believing for arrives. We go from faith to faith, not faith to *feelings.* The Lord has never started anything that He can't finish. So if you have God's Word on something, that Word is the starter and the finisher!

In Matthew 14:30 in the account of Peter walking on the water, why did Peter begin to sink? Because he took his eyes off Jesus, the starter and finisher of his faith.

I always exhort people who are believing God for certain things to stand fast in their believing and to keep their eyes focused on Jesus, the author and finisher of their faith, not on their circumstances. Then their faith will work (I qualify that by whether they have things in order—whether they're living a clean life, tithing and giving offerings and confessing the Word). When they stand fast in faith and are living right, God must bring deliverance in their situations and circumstances.

I've got good news for you if you are believing God. If you are holding fast and continuing to fight the good fight of faith, God is in the process of doing something for you *now!* Here's what you've got to understand. When you're dealing in faith, there is a *timing* for the manifestation. It takes time sometimes for your faith to pull things into the natural realm. That's why the Bible says it's **from faith to faith** (Romans 1:17). You have to stay in faith even when you don't see any changes. In your faith, you have to get above seeing or feeling something.

### FINISH THE FIGHT

I want you to notice something about the apostle Paul from Second Timothy 4:7:

> **I have fought a good fight, I have finished my course, I have kept the faith.**

Notice three things Paul did to finish his fight: (1) *he fought the good fight of faith;* (2) *he finished the course;* and (3) *he kept the faith.* Now, in this context, Paul was talking about coming to the end of life's race, but we can use these same principles in finishing each one of our individual faith fights.

*First,* Paul fought the good fight of faith. The just shall live by faith, so we know that we are to walk by faith in life. *Second,* Paul finished the course. Finished means *completed.* Paul didn't quit halfway through. He *finished* the course. *Third,* Paul kept the faith.

The fact that Paul *kept* the faith implies that there were things that tried to take it away from him. For one, Paul was beaten, whipped and locked in jail in a strange city, Philippi. That could have taken his faith from him, but Paul held on to his faith. He looked over at Silas in that dark prison and said, "Let's sing." And they began to sing. When they did, those prison doors shook open! (See Acts 16:23-26.)

## SATAN IS A DEADLINE DEVIL!

When your faith is challenged, you must fight the good fight of faith. You must stay on course until the fight is finished, and you must keep the faith. Do you remember any faith projects that you didn't finish—that you let go of too soon? It's important to keep the faith and finish the course. I mean, when the dust starts flying, the smoke gets thick and the fire is hot, don't throw in the towel! Finish your course. Keep the faith. The devil is going to say to you, "Do you really believe all that? The situation is getting worse. You're not going to make it." One of his favorite lines is, "You're not going to get your answer in time." He is a deadline devil!

## THE IMPORTANCE OF TIMING IN TESTIFYING

Here's something else about manifestations. Sometimes when we're operating in faith, we cheer too early. We "mouth off" our testimonies too fast, before we truly have the answer. When it comes to sickness and disease, I don't permit my people to testify too quickly after they've been through a major battle. When you testify too soon, the devil hasn't had his turn yet. In other words, when you're dealing with something in the spirit realm and you're winning by faith, the enemy is not just going to roll over and play dead and let you have your answer. He's going to come back and try to put something on you again. When you learn to keep him off you by holding fast to your faith and confession, then you are operating in the kind of faith that receives victory and *maintains* that victory.

Sometimes people get a little victory, and they begin to tell everybody about it. Then the enemy comes back stronger to contend with them, and they're not ready to handle it. But if they would just hold their testimony of the victory within themselves for a while longer and continue to praise God, then in the process of praising Him, they will become stronger. Then when the enemy comes back, they are strong enough to resist him and to refuse to let him back in.

Don't take the sickle out too early when you're operating in faith. What is a sickle used for? A sickle is used for reaping. So, for example, if you're believing God for $10,000, don't shout over the *$1,000* too much. Just hang in there until you get the full manifestation and you are strong enough that 10,000 devils couldn't take that $10,000 away from you!

## DON'T EXAGGERATE YOUR FAITH

Also, some people exaggerate about their faith—actually, they "flat out" lie about it! Some people say they received things by faith, but they really got it through the flesh. Sometimes they got it—especially if it's money or some material substance—through conning people. They stood next to someone who's wealthy and said, for example, "I'm standing in faith for a washing machine. I know the Lord is working on my behalf." They weren't believing God; they were believing for that person to give them a check to go get that washing machine! I don't know why they didn't just go ahead and tell the person, "I need a washing machine. Would you buy me one?"

## LEAVE THE "HOW" UP TO GOD

Now let's look at another reference to God's timing.

66

And he [Jesus] said, So is the kingdom of God, as if a man should cast seed into the ground; And should sleep, and rise night and day, and the seed should spring and grow up, he knoweth not how. For the earth bringeth forth fruit of herself; first the blade, then the ear, after that the full corn in the ear.

MARK 4:26-28

These Scriptures in Mark 4 are an explanation of the Kingdom of God. Notice verses 26 and 27: **And he said, So is the kingdom of God, as if a man should cast seed into the ground; And should sleep, and rise night and day, and the seed should spring and grow up, he** KNOWETH NOT HOW.

You see, it's your responsibility to know that God is *willing*. It is your responsibility to know that God is *able*. But you must leave the "how" up to God. The problem comes when you try to figure out how God is going to perform what you're believing for. Leave it up to God. Those three Hebrew boys in Daniel 3 left it up to God. They said, "We're *outside* of the fire now, and we're not going to serve or bow to you. And if you throw us *inside* the fire, we're *still* not going to serve you, because our God is able!" (See Daniel 3:13-18). They were saying that, one way or the other, God was going to deliver them, because He's able. They knew He was willing and able. But they left the "how" up to God, and God decided to do it in the fire!

What's the difference whether those three Hebrew boys were outside the fire or inside the fire? They were inside the fire, but the fire didn't burn them. The smoke didn't even make them stink, and not one hair on their heads was singed. So what's the difference? I don't mind walking in a fire that doesn't burn! Do you? And, I tell you, some of the things that you think are going to overtake you in life are not going to overtake you. God is going to stop them when the time comes.

67

I want you to thoroughly understand my point about manifestations. It is very important that you leave the "how" up to God. If you are believing God for something right now, do you know that He is *willing?* You should have found that out in the Book. The Bible tells us that He is willing.

The Bible also tells us that He is *able.* Do you know that He is *able?* Then leave the "how" up to God! Just follow the Bible.

You know, some wives have husbands who do not treat them right. If that's your situation, just follow the Bible. Treat that rascal right according to what Peter told you: **Ye wives, be in subjection to your own husbands; that, if any obey not the word, they also may without the word be won by the conversation of the wives; While they behold your chaste conversation coupled with fear** (1 Peter 3:1,2). You do what you're supposed to do and let God handle that husband.

You might find it hard to believe, but there are Christian people in the church, singing and shouting, who go home and treat their mates with no love or respect. You might think that woman in your church who's crying has the power of God all over her. But she may be hurting because her husband standing next to her has both hands in the air, shouting, "Glory to God!" and she knows in her heart that he's a liar.

Also, when you're in a faith fight, you can't stay in a dead church. If you are in a dead church, you need to get out of it. If you want to live in victory but your church is not teaching the fullness of the Holy Ghost and the life of faith, that church is not the place for you. If your church is still teaching man-made tradition and doctrine, although you may be full of the Word from some good teaching book or tape or special meeting, that church would pull that Word right out of you. Some people stay in dead, dry churches because they say, "My mother, my grandmother and my great-grandmother were members of this church." So what! Is *Jesus* there?

### STAY WITH THE WORD AND DON'T GO DOWN WITH ANY SINKING SHIPS!

I have made up my mind that I am not going to sink with any ship. I'm getting off a ship if it's sinking! I'm going to get a life raft—I'm going to get a word from God, and I'm going to get on that word and ride away from that mess! I tell you right now, I am not sinking with any ships. I will not stay with people and ministries that do not want to do right.

I'm so glad I'm not dead anymore. I'm so glad I'm not bound by religion, tradition, philosophy and the doctrines of men. I'm free at last! Glory to God! The Word of God has set me free! Nobody can hold me down. I've got the Word of God living inside of me, working mightily! I'm a winner, because *Jesus* is a winner. And I am in Him. The devil is under my feet. He is a defeated foe.

As I was preaching this message one time, the Lord gave the following word:

> The pathway to God's blessings is not closed. He has opened the way. So enter in. Look not to the left or to the right. There will be voices hollering at you. Answer not those voices, for they are the voices of deceit, religion, tradition, philosophy and the doctrines of men. Keep walking down the pathway of God's Word. There is joy and victory upon that pathway. Continue to walk in the same direction in which you started in faith. Walk by faith and not by sight, and there will come a point in your life, no matter who you are, in which all your needs will be met—and not only your needs, but God will give you your heart's desires and use you mightily in His Kingdom.

You might say, "But you don't understand. I can't read well" or "I have such and such a condition" or "I come from a low-income family."

It makes no difference. If you'll just keep walking down that pathway, God will raise you up, and His richest blessings will be upon you.

## THE BLADE, THE EAR AND THE FULL CORN IN THE EAR

Now let's look at the rest of that passage in Mark 4.

**For the earth bringeth forth fruit of herself; FIRST the BLADE, THEN the EAR, AFTER THAT the FULL CORN IN THE EAR. But when the fruit is brought forth, immediately he putteth in the sickle, because the harvest is come.**

MARK 4:28,29

Notice, in verse 28, it says the fruit (or manifestation) is brought forth—first, the *blade;* then the *ear;* and, after that, the *full corn in the ear. Then* the reaper puts in the sickle, not before. That's why I told you not to try to harvest too soon when you're operating in faith. People are tripping themselves up trying to reap before there's a full manifestation. They get ahold of the faith message, but often, they're trying to live by somebody else's experience. What they need to do is to first go through faith "boot camp." In other words, if they would just take their time and get in the Word for themselves, they would find that faith works!

These three things in verse 28—*first the blade, then the ear,* and *after that the full corn in the ear*—will keep your faith intact and keep you from trying to harvest your manifestation too soon. Too many of us in our faith try to harvest just the blade. But if you harvest the blade, it's not going to last, because it's not the full manifestation of your faith. Then others try to harvest when the ear is manifested. Why don't they just wait for the full corn in the ear?

How many of us at one time have tried to harvest the blade? If you've been in the faith walk very long, you've probably tried to harvest the blade at some time or another. Then the ear looked a little stronger—like you really had everything you were believing for. But the *blade* wasn't it. The *ear* wasn't it. The *full corn in the ear* is the full manifestation. *That* is the time to take out the sickle and reap the harvest of God's blessings!

# Chapter 5

*Locate Your Faith and Move*
*Forward to Victory!*

If you are going to meet the challenges to your faith in life, one of the first things that you're going to have to do is *locate* your faith.

What does it mean to locate your faith? It means to find out where you are in your faith. You need to find out if you have enough faith developed to handle your situation. If you don't, you may need to get somebody to agree with you on that particular challenge. Matthew 18:19 says, **Again I say unto you, That if two of you shall agree on earth as touching any thing that they shall ask, it shall be done for them of my Father which is in heaven.**

You see, you might not be able to deal with a particular problem by yourself. If that happens, fear can come in, and what faith you have developed stops. Fear stops faith. That is where pastoral work comes in—in helping people locate their faith. I don't teach people to believe they've got it all and have no need of anything or anyone else. People who believe they have it *all* had better know how to *call!* In other words, people who think they have perfectly developed faith and can't go any further in their faith had better know how to call other believers for help, because one day they're going to need to.

73

A person who knows when to call is wiser than the person who thinks he can handle it all! A wise person knows where his faith is and knows when he needs to call for help. I tell you, in certain situations in life—especially life or death situations—I'd rather call than to be guessing about it or to be thinking I'm somewhere in my faith that I'm really not.

The Bible talks about different measures and degrees of faith. The Bible talks about *little* faith, *weak* faith, *strong* faith and *great* faith. So since there are different measures of faith, you need to be able to locate your faith. The way to locate your faith is with the Word. In this chapter, I'm going to give you some examples of different measures of faith.

## EVERYONE HAS THE POTENTIAL FOR GREAT FAITH

According to Romans 12:3, God gives every one of His children the measure of faith. But our faith is developed at different rates of progress. It's important that you know this: *Whatever* level your faith is at, your faith *will* be challenged.

Many people do not know where they are in faith; they don't have their faith located. They can talk the talk: "Hey, hey! I've got faith to tear down a mountain." But when a hill shows up, and they say, "Move, hill," it doesn't move. Then they'll say, "Oh, Lord, what am I going to do now?"

I'll tell you what to do. You ask for help; you let somebody else help you move that mountain. At the point that you say, "It didn't move; what am I going to do now?" *you have just located yourself,* because you would never ask that question if you had enough faith to move that hill.

A lot of people read Mark 11:23, which says, **Whosoever shall say unto this mountain, Be thou removed, and be thou cast into the sea; and shall not doubt in his heart, but shall believe that those things which he saith shall come to pass; he shall have whatsoever**

**he saith,** and they think they've got mountain-moving faith. But you don't know whether you have mountain-moving faith until the mountain shows up! When the mountain shows up, are you going to scream out in terror, or are you going to move the mountain?

## FAITH MUST BE EXERCISED AND DEVELOPED

Just *saying* you have mountain-moving faith does not give you the faith to move mountains. Certainly, God has given you the measure of faith, but you have to use and develop your measure of faith. To have mountain-moving faith, you have to have some experience moving mountains!

When you are dealing with big things—mountains—you have to know that they do not always move fast. When you are dealing with a mountain, brother and sister, it takes some force to move that thing. It's not that it can't be moved, but it isn't going to be moved by just saying, "Verily, verily, I say unto you, be moved, mountain." No, mountains do not dissipate that quickly.

You have to look that mountain straight in the eye, lock your feet down and tell the mountain, "I am not going to move until you move." Sometimes you have to stay right there a good while. Sometimes your faith will be challenged. So get ahold of that mountain and tell it to *move!* When you have tenacious, mountain-moving faith, there is no limit to what you can be and do. You will just look your mountain in the eye and dare it not to move!

Some people want *God* to move the mountains out of their lives. But you have to learn how to develop and use your own faith.

## LITTLE FAITH

Now let's look at some Scriptures that will help us locate our faith.

> And straightway Jesus constrained his disciples to get into a ship, and to go before him unto the other side, while he sent the multitudes away. And when he had sent the multitudes away, he went up into a mountain apart to pray: and when the evening was come, he was there alone. But the ship was now in the midst of the sea, tossed with waves: for the wind was contrary.
>
> MATTHEW 14:22-24

Verse 24 says, **The wind was contrary.** And, you know, some contrary wind is going to come to *your* life at one time or another to challenge your faith. Do you remember what Jesus said in Matthew 7:24-25?

> Therefore whosoever heareth these sayings of mine, and doeth them, I will liken him unto a wise man, which built his house upon a rock: And the rain descended, and the floods came, and the winds blew, and beat upon that house; and it fell not: for it was founded upon a rock.

Could you say that the rain, the floods and the winds in verse 25 were *challenges?* You see, Jesus told these stories for a reason. He used everyday things to get our attention; but actually, in this passage, He was talking about the adversities of life. Things in this life and in this world will try to come against you. He said, "If you are a doer of the Word, let the rain fall, the floods come and the winds blow; but you'll stand, because you are founded upon a rock."

Have you ever had any rain, floods or winds in your life? Sure you have. Adversities come against us all. Sometimes they're like hurricanes—wind blowing, water falling and people running! But it's how you handle adversities that counts. Are you going to stand there, or are you going to run with the others? If you start running with the crowd, you are not going to develop faith to move the mountains of adversity.

76

## "LITTLE FAITH" RUNS FROM PROBLEMS

Some people run from everything. A little trouble comes into the church, and they will go join another church. I call them "the running bunch"! They don't want to be bothered with life. They'll say, "I don't want no mess." But if they found a church that never had any disturbances, they'd be in heaven!

I really have a hard time respecting somebody who runs from a challenge. I am personally not out looking for challenges, but they find me anyway! And I won't run. I stand and fight the good fight of faith. And my faith is my victory (1 John 5:4)!

The rain is going to fall anyway, whether you hide or not. You could go hide in a hole, but at some point, the rain is going to find you in that hole! The storms of life will find you, so you might as well stay out in the open and let them come.

"Well, what am I going to do when they come?" you might ask. Stand against them! Locate your faith, and use the faith you've developed to resist them! I tell you, you can't always just depend on a corporate anointing when you get to church. Don't always shout on credit—on someone else's faith. You need to learn to stand when you are by yourself. You can't always wait until you get to church. You need to have power at your house, in your car and wherever you are. The devil ought to know who you are. Don't be like the seven sons of Sceva who tried to cast a devil out of someone. That devil said to them, *"Jesus* I know; *Paul* I know; but who are *you?"* (Acts 19:15).

Let's pick up where we left off reading in Matthew 14.

**And in the fourth watch of the night Jesus went unto them, walking on the sea. And when the disciples saw him walking on the sea, they were troubled, saying, It is a spirit; and they cried out for fear. But straightway Jesus spake unto them, saying, Be of good cheer; it is I; be not afraid.**

And Peter answered him and said, Lord, if it be thou, bid me come unto thee on the water. And he said, Come. And when Peter was come down out of the ship, he walked on the water, to go to Jesus. But when he saw the wind boisterous, he was afraid; and beginning to sink, he cried, saying, Lord, save me. And immediately Jesus stretched forth his hand, and caught him, and said unto him, O thou of LITTLE FAITH, wherefore didst thou doubt?

MATTHEW 14:25-31

Now, one of the principles I shared with you previously was that of certifying your faith and refusing to look to the flesh when your faith is challenged. Peter looked to the flesh and at circumstances instead of looking to the Lord, and he began to sink as a result. His faith was what held him up on that water; but when he saw the "wind boisterous," he traded his faith for flesh, and the challenge got ahold of him and began to overcome him. But, at least Peter had the good spiritual sense to cry out to Jesus for help! Some people are "going down" in their circumstances, and they don't want to call anybody. At least Peter did something. He cried out, "Lord, save me!" The Bible says, **And immediately Jesus stretched forth his hand, and caught him, and said unto him, O thou of little faith, wherefore didst thou doubt? (v. 31).**

You see, the Lord dealt with Peter too. Jesus was saying, in effect, "Peter, you didn't need Me to do this. If you had gone on your own faith and kept with it, you could have stayed on top of that water. I'm doing this because you called on Me. You wouldn't have needed to if only you would have recognized the wind and the waves as a challenge to your faith."

So in Matthew 14:31, we read about *little* faith. What is "little faith"? Little faith is what causes you to sink when the adversities of life come against you. The adversities of life came against Peter. He was out there walking on the water. And as long as everything was going all right, with no wind or waves, Peter used his faith; and his faith got certain results. But when a little something came up in his life to shake him up, he began focusing on that, and he began to lose his results. He began to sink.

## YOUR "LITTLE FAITH" CAN GROW!

"Little faith" can't handle the challenge. You need some help. You need to get somebody to help you by agreeing with you in prayer. There is no shame in that at all, as long as you go on to develop your faith more and more. You shouldn't have little faith over the long haul—for the rest of your life.

Also, little faith is complaining and allowing yourself to become depressed and discouraged about what you see or feel. Little faith will not carry you very far on the waters of life, because the wind is going to blow. You have to be able to look at the wind and not see it as bigger than Jesus. You have to be able to talk to the wind and tell it to be still.

## WEAK FAITH

Now let's talk about *weak* faith.

**And being not WEAK in faith, he [Abraham] considered not his own body now dead, when he was about an hundred years old, neither yet the deadness of Sara's womb.**

ROMANS 4:19

Now, Abraham was not weak in faith, but this verse shows us how weak faith operates. Weak faith considers the adversities and challenges to be bigger than God and His Word. Weak faith considers something God has told you to be impossible. With weak faith,

79

you are "considering" circumstances, but when you are operating in *strong* faith, there are some things you have to learn to "consider *not.*"

When we were building our new church building, the devil told me, "Oh, so you're going to build a new church in Darrow? There are no more than 300 people in Darrow, and 95 percent of them don't believe in what you are doing."

You know, the devil laughed at me. "Ha! You're in full-time ministry in *Darrow.* Ha, ha, ha!" I could have started crying and said: "You're right, Mr. Devil. Darrow is nowhere. I need to move to the nearest city—Gonzales or Baton Rouge."

But, no. I "considered not" all the accusations that were made against this ministry nor all the people who said it couldn't be done. And I considered God and His Word. I held fast to my confession of faith and withstood the challenges. The devil brought all kinds of opposition. I wish I could pull my diary out and show you some of the ways the devil tried to stop me. But I considered him not.

## DON'T BLAME PEOPLE OR CIRCUMSTANCES

When you get a word from God, you don't consider anything else. Someone said, "Well, my husband just won't act right." What did the Lord tell you about it? Who are you going to consider—the Lord or your husband?

Someone said, "Well, my wife just won't act right. One of these days I am going to get it straight with You, Lord, but this *woman* You gave me!" No, it's not the woman. It's *you. You* get right with the Lord. You're going to end up with weak faith if you're going to consider the woman.

Someone else said, "Lord, when I get a better job, I'll serve You better." That is like calling the doctor and saying, "When I get better, I am coming to see you"!

You see, weak faith considers everything but God. But Abraham had strong faith. He considered not his own body. He didn't even consider Sarah's body, because the Lord had told him what was going to happen. Sarah was going to have a baby. I don't care how dead her womb was, the Lord had *made* her womb, and Abraham chose to believe Him. He refused to have weak faith!

Weak faith considers the things that you are up against to be stronger than God. God has said, **Lo, I am with you alway, even unto the end of the world** (Matthew 28:20). If you are weak in faith, then, really, you are coming against the Word of God. You are coming against "Lo, I am with you always." The Lord didn't say, "Lo, I am with you when you are in church." No, He said He was with you *always.* So we must not come against the Word and the promises of God if we are to be strong in faith.

## ⟶ STRONG FAITH ⟵

Now notice, verses 20 and 21 talk about the kind of faith Abraham had—*strong* faith. As I said, weak faith considers the problem and not the solution. *Strong* faith considers the solution and not the problem!

He [Abraham] **staggered not at the promise of God through unbelief; but was strong in faith, giving glory to God; And being fully persuaded, that, what he had promised, he was able also to perform.**

ROMANS 4:20,21

These verses show us what strong faith is. First, we remember from verse 19 that Abraham considered not the deadness of Sarah's womb. He considered not the circumstances. Then verse 20 says, **He staggered not at the promise of God.**

So the *first* characteristic of strong faith is *considering not the circumstances.* The *second* characteristic of strong faith is *staggering not at the promises of God.* (Conversely, staggering at the promises of God is a characteristic of *weak* faith. One day, you're in faith, believing and confessing; the next day you're crying and in doubt. That's weak faith.)

Do you know what "stagger" means? Have you ever seen someone who's drunk? A drunk person usually doesn't know where he is. He staggers in his mind; he is confused. He staggers when he walks. He doesn't have any stability at all.

When *we* stagger at the promises of God, we are confused. We don't have any stability to stand our ground—to stand firmly in one place on the Word of God and declare that God's Word is true.

In Romans 4:20, the example of Abraham demonstrates strong faith: **He staggered not at the promise of God through unbelief; but was strong in faith, giving glory to God.** Abraham was giving glory to God. Abraham didn't waver concerning God's promise, and he gave glory to God.

You see, faith honors and glorifies God, and God honors faith. When you begin to walk strong in faith and give glory to God, He will cross over two million people just to get to you and bless you!

We are missing a lot of things in life because we have not considered God as God. It is hard to find people who will really commit themselves to God and trust Him. But He is looking for those persons—those who will give Him glory—and when He finds them, He raises them up. And nobody can hold them down when God raises them up!

That is thoroughly scriptural. Look at Second Chronicles 16:9: **For the eyes of the Lord run to and fro throughout the whole earth, to shew himself strong in the behalf of them whose heart is perfect toward him.**

## ⸻ IS GOD LOOKING FOR *YOU?* ⸻

The eyes of the Lord run to and fro, looking for somebody who is going to stand on His Word until that Word becomes a tug that defies gravity, so to speak, and lifts him up above and beyond everything that tries to hold him down. God is looking for somebody to honor Him with strong faith. Is it going to be you? Are you going to be one of those whom God is looking for?

God is looking for somebody to sell out to Him, to fight the good fight of faith and to lay hold on eternal life. We have been called to give God a good name by living right and by dealing with the adversities of life according to His Word, by standing on His promises and receiving supernatural results!

God wants to be shown strong, because He *is* strong. There is not a person anywhere whom God wouldn't raise up. Just begin to show Him strong. Exalt and glorify Him with strong faith, considering not your circumstances and staggering not at the promises of God.

God is looking for somebody to bless more and more. But He is not going to bless you if you're complaining, griping, talking about folks and trying to hold folks down. So just go ahead and do what He told you to do in His Word, and He will bless you.

There are people who are blessed continually because they are following the plan of God for their lives, but let me tell you, their faith will still be challenged. No matter where you are in your faith walk—whether you have weak or strong faith—your faith is going to be challenged. You have to learn to locate your faith so you can meet the challenge.

## ⸻ GREAT FAITH ⸻

Now let's look at Matthew 8 and a case of what Jesus Himself called *great* faith.

> And when Jesus was entered into Capernaum, there came unto him a centurion, beseeching him, And saying, Lord, my servant lieth at home sick of the palsy, grievously tormented. And Jesus saith unto him, I will come and heal him. The centurion answered and said, Lord, I am not worthy that thou shouldest come under my roof: but speak the word only, and my servant shall be healed. For I am a man under authority, having soldiers under me: and I say to this man, Go, and he goeth; and to another, Come, and he cometh; and to my servant, Do this, and he doeth it. When Jesus heard it, he marvelled, and said to them that followed, Verily I say unto you, I have not found so GREAT FAITH, no, not in Israel.

Jesus said that this centurion had great faith. *Great faith* is faith that leans on the Word and the Word only. In verse 8, the centurion said to Jesus, **Speak the word only, and my servant shall be healed.**

Another characteristic of great faith is that *it will not take no for an answer.* We can see that characteristic in the woman of Canaan in Matthew 15.

> Then Jesus went thence, and departed into the coasts of Tyre and Sidon. And, behold, a woman of Canaan came out of the same coasts, and cried unto him, saying, Have mercy on me, O Lord, thou Son of David; my daughter is grievously vexed with a devil. But he answered her not a word. And his disciples came and besought him, saying, Send her away; for she crieth after us. But he answered and said, I am not sent but unto the lost sheep of the house of Israel. Then came she and worshipped him, saying, Lord, help me. But he answered and said, It is not meet to take the children's bread, and to cast it to dogs. And she said, Truth, Lord: yet the dogs eat of the crumbs which fall from their

masters' table. **Then Jesus answered and said unto her, O woman, GREAT IS THY FAITH: be it unto thee even as thou wilt. And her daughter was made whole from that very hour.**

MATTHEW 15:21-28

Great faith will not take no for an answer. In other words, great faith already has the answer. This woman of Canaan had tenacity and boldness. She had a "stick with it" type of faith. Jesus called it *great* faith.

Look at verse 23: **But he [Jesus] answered her not a word....**

The woman was crying after Jesus, asking Him to help her, and He answered her not a word!

## DON'T TAKE NO FOR AN ANSWER!

What would you have done? Most people probably would have left and said, "This Jesus mess doesn't work." We are so used to all this instant stuff—fast food, fast service, fast *everything*. We want what we want, and we want it *right now!* But notice how this woman persisted.

After Jesus **answered her not a word,** He said, **I am not sent but unto the lost sheep of the house of Israel** (v. 24). What was Jesus saying? Basically, He was saying, "Girl, you don't even qualify. You are the wrong nationality."

Then it says she **worshipped him, saying, Lord, help me** (v. 25). But Jesus answered, **It is not meet to take the children's bread, and to cast it to dogs** (v. 26).

What did she do? She said, **Truth, Lord: yet the dogs eat of the crumbs which fall from their masters' table** (v. 27). This woman was not going to take no for an answer!

85

When Jesus saw her faith, He said, **O woman, great is thy faith: be it unto thee even as thou wilt. And her daughter was made whole from that very hour** (v. 28).

I showed you some different levels and degrees of faith from the Word so you could see that your faith can be at any one of these levels at any given time. In other words, just because you have strong faith or great faith today doesn't necessarily mean you're going to have that kind of faith down the road somewhere. Developing your faith is a continual, everyday process. If you lag in the development of your faith, you could become cold. If your mind is not continually being renewed, your faith will not operate as effectively as it did at some point in the past.

This faith walk is a never-ending process. You should never become complacent in your faith. You should be growing daily, having ever-increasing faith. The more you know about God's Word, the more you should want to know. You have to keep studying. It's not a one-time shot. You have to keep renewing your mind every day. You have to keep going forward. You have to forget the things that are behind you—your victories as well as your failures, the compliments as well as the criticisms. Put them all in one sack, so to speak, and forget about them while you go forward and continue to fight the good fight of faith, laying hold on victory and eternal life.

# Chapter 6

## *How To Convert* Contests *Into* Conquests!

We need to know how to deal with the challenges of life properly so that we can turn our natural circumstances into supernatural victories—so that we can turn the power of the enemy over to the power of God. The power of God always supersedes the power of the enemy.

We do have an enemy, and we are in a contest. According to Second Corinthians 4:4, the enemy, Satan, is called the god of this world. But he is not *our* god if we are born again. And when we learn our rights and learn how to walk by faith, we can turn our enemy to flight. He'll run from us. But as long as we are ignorant of our rights in Christ, the enemy always will have us on the run.

We ought to aim to turn this run around. We are not going to run from the enemy. We are going to run behind him, keeping *him* on the move. It's our responsibility to keep Satan out of our lives.

The Father God has made it possible for the Church, which represents Him in the earth, to take authority over every situation that may come against us. But we cannot do it ignorantly. We have to do it by being knowledgeable of the things of God and by applying that knowledge.

When you begin to understand in your heart, not just your head, your rights in Christ, and you begin to lay hold on the benefits He has provided you, sickness cannot override you. Poverty cannot overtake you. As I said before, it won't happen automatically. It is a fight. But you can learn to walk with God in such a way that you win all the time.

Now, in some particular contests or challenges, sometimes the fight goes five or six rounds. You have to understand that. It might go twelve rounds. It might go *fifteen* rounds.

"Well," somebody said, "even the heavyweight championship is over in fifteen rounds." But *your* fight is not over until you win! If you are staying in the fight with the Word of God and that fight doesn't end in fifteen rounds, the Father God will extend it to twenty rounds if He needs to—whatever it takes for you to win!

## Converting Tests to Triumphs Is for *Here*, Not the *Hereafter*

We have been taught that all of our victories will be complete in heaven. When this life on earth is all over and we have crossed over the threshold, *that* is when we are really going to start living. No! I want to tell you, we are going to start living *today!* We are going to learn how to convert the contests of life to conquests!

Have you ever heard the word "convert" or "conversion" in a church setting? In the natural, we derive the word "convertible," referring to an automobile, from the word *convert.* With a convertible, you can change the appearance of that car from a car *with* a top on it to a car *without* a top on it. In other words, that car is converted from one appearance to another.

When we got saved, we became converted from one species to another—from sinner to saint! We were converted by the Converter, and we became new creatures in Christ (2 Corinthians 5:17).

In the Scripture we are about to read, we are going to find out how to convert from the natural to the supernatural every situation that comes against your faith. We can convert every contest into a conquest—from the power of Satan to the power of God.

> For this people's heart is waxed gross, and their EARS are dull of hearing, and their EYES they have closed; lest at any time they should SEE WITH THEIR EYES, and HEAR WITH THEIR EARS, and should UNDERSTAND WITH THEIR HEART, and should be CONVERTED, and I should heal them.
>
> MATTHEW 13:15

We are not going to look at the negative connotation of this Scripture. There is a positive aspect to this verse, too, and it can change your life. It can change the way you fight life's battles.

The first part of Matthew 13:15 says, **For this people's heart is waxed gross, and their ears are dull of hearing, and their eyes they have closed....** That is the negative aspect, but I want to show you something from the positive aspect that will help you deal with things in your life when your faith is challenged.

—∞— THE FIRST STEP: —∞—
HAVING EYES THAT SEE

The rest of that verse says, **...lest at any time they should see with their eyes, and hear with their ears, and should understand with their heart, and should be converted....**

Look at that phrase **lest at any time they should see with their eyes.** That is the first step in converting a challenging situation: You have to have eyes that see. You have to see with the eyes of your spirit. You have to see revelation knowledge. When you begin to see revelation in the Word of God, you begin to see beyond the situation that is staring you in the face. You begin to see God as bigger than any problem. You can dance, shout and jump in the midst of the problem. Having eyes that can see spiritual things will put you in a good position to convert your *contests* to *conquests.*

Now, if you have not been taught about this before, you might say, "What do you mean by 'eyes that can see'? I have eyes, and I can see." But, really, you have two sets of eyes—the eyes of your natural man and the eyes of your spirit.

John 4:24 says, **God is a Spirit: and they that worship him must worship him in spirit and in truth.** We could substitute the word "understand" for *worship,* and say it like this: "They that *understand* Him must *understand* Him in spirit and in truth." We could also say, "They that walk with Him must walk with Him in spirit and in truth." You see, your fellowship with God is a spiritual transaction.

## LEARN TO SEE THINGS FROM GOD'S POINT OF VIEW

With the eyes of the spirit, you see revelation knowledge from the Word of God. And in order to convert your contest, or challenge, when you are in a faith fight, you are going to have to be able to see your way out of it! You are going to have to see your way past the problem and focus on the answer!

Now, the Bible says that we walk by faith, not by sight (2 Corinthians 5:7), but I am talking about another kind of sight here. I'm talking about spiritual sight—about seeing things like God sees them—through the eyes of God, so to speak.

I dare you today to see your situation through the eyes of God! How does God see things? Well, if you are sick, see yourself well. See the fact that **He [Jesus] was wounded for our transgressions, he was bruised for our iniquities: the chastisement of our peace was upon him; and with his stripes we are healed** (Isaiah 53:5). See that

**Himself took our infirmities, and bare our sicknesses** (Matthew 8:17). See that **His own self bare our sins in his own body on the tree, that we, being dead to sins, should live unto righteousness: by whose stripes ye were healed** (1 Peter 2:24).

That is what it means to see with the eyes of God. That is how God sees—in line with His Word! When our faith is challenged, instead of seeing just with our *physical* eyes, we need to learn how to see with our *spiritual* eyes.

So the first thing you need to do to convert contests into conquests is to train yourself to see things from God's point of view. Instead of looking in the natural at how bad things may seem, you need to see revelation knowledge from the Word of God. The Lord will show you how to get out of that situation and overcome it. But you're going to have to see correctly to receive the revelation—to see what He is showing you.

Some people have never seen anything spiritually. They have not been trained properly. Did you know that you could go around quoting, **The Lord is my shepherd; I shall not want,** and be in want all the days of your life? You could be sixty-five years old and still be in want. You're quoting Psalm 23:1 all right, but you haven't *seen* it yet. It has not become a reality to you. If that verse in Psalm 23 had become a reality to you, over a period of time, something would have started happening to you. The Lord would have become your Shepherd, and your wants would have started leaving!

There are other ramifications to confessing Scripture to receive your needs. For example, you could be saying, "The Lord is my Shepherd. I shall not want." But the Lord could be saying to you in another verse, "Do this" or "Don't do that," and you're saying, "Well, I don't want to obey that. I don't want to hear that part. I think I'll skip that page."

If that's the case, your confession, "The Lord is my Shepherd. I shall not want," will not work for you, because you are dissecting the Scriptures the way *you* want to follow them. You're not following the full program of God. I mean, if He starts talking to you about tithing and giving, and you say, "Well, I don't want to do that," you aren't being willing and obedient to the full program. And you don't qualify for the promise "The Lord is my Shepherd. I shall not want." So when you tear out the page of the Bible that contains Malachi 3:10, which talks about tithing, you're going to have to tear out Psalm 23 too!

## THE SECOND STEP:
### HAVING EARS THAT HEAR

Now let's look at the second step to converting your contests into conquests. First, we need to look again at Matthew 13:15:

> **...lest at any time they should see with their eyes, and HEAR WITH THEIR EARS, and should understand with their heart, and should be converted....**

The second thing you have to have if you want to convert a situation are ears to hear spiritual things. It always amazes me how four people can be sitting in the same row in church, and three of them don't hear anything the preacher is saying! I'm talking about spiritual things. They don't hear with their spiritual ears. They say, "What's going on? I'm tired; I'm ready to go." And all the while, the Lord is trying to get their attention and help them change their situations!

You can be dull of hearing and close off what God is saying to you. God will speak to you and minister to you if you will let Him. But you could think, *I'm not going to listen to that preacher because he's a black man,* and close yourself off to what God is trying to teach you.

Or you could say, "Well, I'm just visiting this church with my friend. As soon as this service is over, I'm going home, and that's it.

I'm not coming back. They're too wild in this church. I don't like all that jumping and shouting and hollering. I want to leave." You might even sense the presence of God and get blessed a little. But you can be dull of hearing if you don't humble yourself, purpose to be teachable and hear what the Spirit of God is saying to you personally.

Many people do not have ears to hear, and that is why they are all mixed up in life. They don't even know when the Spirit of God is moving. But when you have ears to hear what the Spirit of God is saying to you, He will begin to convert your situation. He will begin to stop the confusion in your house. He will bring peace, joy and love.

"But how fast will He do it?" someone may ask. It might be over a protracted period of time. But if you keep standing strong in the Word and staying humble and teachable to hear the Spirit of God, God will never fail you.

## STEP THREE: HAVING A HEART TO UNDERSTAND

God wants us to have understanding concerning His will for our lives, and He has given us the means to obtain understanding through His Word. Now, as I said before, in order to understand the Lord, you have to understand Him in your *heart,* not just in your head.

Look at Ephesians 5.

**Wherefore be ye not unwise, but understanding what the will of the Lord is.**

EPHESIANS 5:17

In order to understand what the will of the Lord is, you are going to have to have eyes that see spiritually, ears that hear spiritually and a heart that can understand spiritual things. Once you become a child of God, you are in a position to walk in these avenues, but it is going to take time. You have to exercise, train and develop your spirit. And you have to be teachable. You can't be a know-it-all and be sensitive

93

to the things of God at the same time. Sometimes you are going to be corrected, and you have to be able to take it. And sometimes you are going to be tempted to be hurt or offended. You have to be able to do the *right* thing when you are tempted to do the *wrong* thing.

When you have eyes that see, ears that hear and a heart to understand, you will be in position to withstand and overcome the challenges of life. If something comes against you, you already know what the will of the Lord is. You know that Jesus has redeemed you. You know your benefits in Him. You know that greater is He that is in you than he that is in the world (1 John 4:4). You know that God is on your side and that if He is for you, who can be against you (Romans 8:31)? You know that your situation is not the will of the Lord. You know that the will of God for you is victory.

And you know what to do! You know that all things are possible to him who believes (Mark 9:23). You know that faith is the victory that overcomes the world (1 John 5:4). You know that you should count it all joy when you fall into various tests, trials and temptations (James 1:2). And on top of that, you know what the outcome will be! You know that you are coming out of that situation by faith.

So you keep applying the pressure of the Word, speaking forth what the Word says about the situation, staying in agreement and fellowship with God. You know that if you are in agreement with God, then God, the One who knows no impossibilities, will make it possible for you to win.

When you have eyes to see, ears to hear and a heart to understand what the will of the Lord is, others will take notice of you. They will say about you, "He's going through a test. How is he able to take it the way he's taking it?" But you can take it because you have inside information! You are looking at that test, not with your natural eyes, but with the eyes of your spirit—with the eyes of faith. You are hearing with spiritual ears, and you are understanding with your heart. You know that this test is only temporary and that God is bringing you out!

You need to confess out loud, "I have eyes that see and ears that hear. I am going to see revelation knowledge in God's Word. I am going to hear what God is saying to me. And I have a heart to understand. I am not unwise concerning the will of the Lord, but I fully understand God's will in my situations and circumstances. I will not sit down and cry, asking, 'Why me?' The Lord is in me, and whatever I go through, He is with me. He is in it too! If I go down, He will have to go down. If I lose, He will have to lose! And God never loses!"

You see, your physical eyes, your physical ears and your physical heart are not sufficient in spiritual things. There is a spirit man inside of you, and he has supernatural eyes and ears and a supernatural heart. As you feed that man on the inside with the Word of God, your mind becomes renewed, and you begin to think in line with that inner man— you begin to think the thoughts of God. Let me ask you a question. Does God ever think He is going to lose? Does God ever think He is going to be defeated in any way? No! God cannot even think of losing; and when we get our minds renewed, we will not think of losing, either.

The world will think you're crazy when your mind becomes renewed to think like God thinks. They will not know where you are coming from. Where *are* you coming from? Out of your inner man! You are speaking spiritual things; they are speaking natural things. They are only dealing with addition, so to speak. But you are dealing with multiplication, because you are dealing with God!

## DON'T GET STALLED IN COMBAT!

You see, in the midst of a test or trial, without renewing your mind—without operating in revelation knowledge—you will get stalled in combat. Satan is going to put a lot of things out there for you to see with your natural eyes, and he will try to get your attention on those things in the natural. That is what happened to Peter in Matthew 14:30 when he was walking on the water. Satan put up a lot of things for Peter to see and hear, such as the thrashing of the water and the whistling of the wind. And Peter got his eyes off the revelation—off Jesus walking on the water. Once Peter lost that revelation, he lost his ability to defy gravity, and he began to sink.

You see, as long as Peter was looking at Jesus, he was looking at the revelation that it was possible for him to walk on water! He had his eyes on that revelation.

The water or the winds make no difference for someone who is walking by revelation knowledge. When you see the revelation, you are seeing Jesus, and whatever He does, you can do. I can prove that with the Bible.

> **Verily, verily, I say unto you, He that believeth on me, the works that I do SHALL HE DO ALSO; and greater works than these shall he do; because I go unto my Father.**
>
> JOHN 14:12

Jesus was saying, in effect, "The works that I do shall he do also, and I'm going to see to it that he's able to do them."

So if somebody hollers at you, "Hey, nobody has ever walked on water before—this situation is going to take you down!" you can say, "Yes, but I have eyes that see and ears that hear, and I have a heart that understands. I understand that I can change the natural into the supernatural. This situation came against me, and I am going against it in the power of God. God is going to make the impossible possible to me because I am born again. I'm converted, and I am going to convert this situation and turn it around in my favor. I'm going to convert this *contest* into a *conquest!*"

The words "I can't" should be taken out of your vocabulary. As you begin to yield to the Spirit of God and get in line with God's

Word, you *can* win! "Yeah," someone may say, "but you don't know my situation." I do not need to know your situation. I am telling you something that can get you out of *any* situation. Whatever your situation is, it can be converted by the Word of God. It can be changed. With eyes that see and ears that hear and a heart that understands, everything in your life that is not in line with God's will can be changed. Problems can be converted. Sickness can be converted. Poverty can be converted. Everything can come in line with and convert to the will of God.

## From Convert to Converter

The exciting part of this revelation is that when you become a Christian, you not only become a convert, but you become a *converter!* You yourself become a converter of situations and circumstances, because now you are walking in the realm of the supernatural. You have God's kind of faith. You have ears that hear, eyes that see and a heart that understands. You have the ability to speak to a circumstance and tell it to change, and God will say, "I will do it. I will perform it for him!"

Look at Matthew 13:15 again: **For this people's heart is waxed gross, and their ears are dull of hearing, and their eyes they have closed; lest at any time they should see with their eyes, and hear with their ears, and should understand with their heart, and should be converted, and I should heal them.**

When you become a convert, you get in position for God to move and do the impossible in your life. Notice the last part of that verse: **...and I should heal them.** Instead of using that word "heal," we could fill in the blank without doing harm to the verse, because it is a principle. In other words, we could say, "...and I should *prosper*

97

them." Or, "...and I should *resolve the problem*." Or, "...and I should *bring the answer to pass*"!

So when you become a convert—when you become saved—you get in position for God to move in your life. But you have to have eyes to see, ears to hear and a heart to understand. Then when you are confronted by a situation, you will know what to do, and you will know what God will do for you.

## LEARN TO DISCERN DARKNESS FROM LIGHT

Some people do not know the difference between God's plans and the work of the devil. For example, they get sick, and they will say, "God is trying to teach me something." No! God is not the author of sickness. The Bible says that all sickness is a curse of the law (Deuteronomy 28:61). You have to have eyes to see, ears to hear and a heart to understand that the devil is the power of darkness, and God is the power of light. If there is darkness in a situation, you can know that it is not God. So just see what God's Word says, hear what God is saying and have some understanding in your heart, and God will convert that thing. He will move the situation for you from the kingdom of darkness to the Kingdom of light.

Let's look at Matthew 13:15 again and get some background information on it:

> **For this people's heart is waxed gross, and their ears are dull of hearing, and their eyes they have closed; lest at any time they should see with their eyes, and hear with their ears, and should understand with their heart, and should be converted, and I should heal them.**

Basically, Jesus is speaking here about the people of Israel. If the people of Israel would have seen with their eyes, heard with their ears and understood with their hearts that Jesus is the Converter, He

98

would have converted them. But, you know, Jesus is not just the Converter to convert men from being hell-bound to being heaven-bound; He is the Converter in every realm and aspect of life. His Word is the catalyst that will change anything in your life that you need to have changed. But you have to see the Word with your spiritual eyes, you have to hear it with your spiritual ears; you have to understand it spiritually. Then stand back and let God go with it!

## BAD HABITS CAN BE CONVERTED

Getting in agreement with God and staying in agreement with Him will absolutely put you over the top in the tests and trials of life. What are you doing when you are agreeing with God? You are saying the same thing He says.

Someone might say, "Yeah, but I have this certain habit, and I just can't break it." Then convert it! "How do I do that?" By having eyes to see, ears to hear and a heart to understand that nothing on the outside can control you! Whatever you can name—whether it be dope, cigarettes or alcohol—it cannot control you.

If you have been bound by any of those habits, call the habit by name and say, "You are not going to control me anymore! You have been ruining my life. You've been trying to eat up my body—my brain, my lungs and my liver. You're trying to ruin my family. But I take authority over you. You are on the outside. You are not in my spirit. *God* is in my spirit. As a matter of fact, you can't even talk or think. The only power you have is the power people give you. But I have a mind—the mind of Christ! I can think. And I know that you are powerless. You can't even come off the shelf until I tell you to! I can burst you open and pour you down the drain. You can't pour *me* down the drain, yet I've been *letting* you pour me down the drain. But I'm going to convert this situation today! Nothing can stop me. No habit can break me down and keep me under its control, in Jesus' Name!"

Do not let habits and bondages hold you back from the blessings of God. Live a clean and holy life. Consecrate yourself. The prophets of old—Isaiah, Jeremiah, Ezekiel and others—would go before the people and say, "Consecrate yourselves before God!" We do not hear a lot about consecration in our society today. But consecration is an important part of walking in the blessings of God and overcoming the challenges of life that would try to rob you of those blessings. So strip away those things that are causing you not to bring glory to God's Name.

When Jesus came on the scene, He said, "I am the way, the truth and the life. No man comes to the Father but by Me. I am the bread of life. He that eats My body and drinks My blood shall never hunger or thirst again. I am the light. I am the enlightenment, the understanding. I am the revelation of God to the world."

Do you really know Jesus? He has already told us who He is. But so many Christians are hopping around to different churches. They are having church when they should let the *Church* have *them*. They should become solid members of the Body of Christ who really know Jesus—who have eyes that see, ears that hear and hearts that understand. They should let the Savior, the Head of the Church, have free course and free rein in their lives.

## CONVERSION BEGINS WITH A REVELATION

Now, just because you hear this kind of message or read this book doesn't mean you are going to be able to convert all your challenges overnight. The minute you accept Christ as Savior, you are spiritually converted. But, sometimes, in handling the challenges of life, there is a conversion period. It takes more than one day. It might take more than one *week,* but if you keep the pressure on, finally that "water will change to wine"—the *good* kind of wine, the *Lord's* wine! God will change your natural situation into the supernatural—your impossible situation into the possible!

Let's continue reading in Matthew.

> **And when his disciples were come to the other side, they had forgotten to take bread. Then Jesus said unto them, Take heed and beware of the leaven of the Pharisees and of the Sadducees. And they reasoned among themselves, saying, It is because we have taken no bread. Which when Jesus perceived, he said unto them, O ye of little faith, why reason ye among yourselves, because ye have brought no bread? Do ye yet not understand, neither remember the five loaves of the five thousand, and how many baskets ye took up?**
>
> **Neither the seven loaves of the four thousand, and how many baskets ye took up? HOW IS IT THAT YE DO NOT UNDERSTAND...?**
>
> MATTHEW 16:5-11

Previously, in Matthew, Jesus had performed a miracle by feeding the 5,000 with only two fishes and five loaves of bread (Matthew 14:17-21). So in Matthew 16:6, where Jesus said, **Take heed and beware of the leaven of the Pharisees and of the Sadducees,** He couldn't have been talking about natural bread. He wasn't talking about the fact that the disciples didn't have any bread. He was trying to teach them something, but they didn't understand.

REVELATION KNOWLEDGE ALWAYS
SUPERSEDES SIGNS AND WONDERS

Let's read some background verses in Matthew 16.

> The Pharisees also with the Sadducees came, and tempting desired him that he would shew them a sign from heaven. He answered and said unto them, When it is evening, ye say, It will be fair weather: for the sky is red. And in the morning, It will be foul weather to day: for the sky is red and lowering. O ye hypocrites, ye can discern the face of the sky; but can ye not discern the signs of the times? A wicked and adulterous generation seeketh after a sign; and there shall no sign be given unto it, but the sign of the prophet Jonas. And he left them, and departed.
>
> MATTHEW 16:1-4

One thing Jesus was saying in His conversation with the disciples was that outward signs may change, but revelation remains the same! He was also saying, "Revelation always supersedes signs!"

There are so many Christians who are constantly running behind preachers who operate in the gifts of the Spirit. Christians will fly all over the world just to see somebody operating in the gifts of the Spirit. But not many are running behind revelation! But, you see, revelation supersedes signs. A person ministering to you is one thing, but knowing how to minister to yourself is another thing altogether. Knowing how to face life's challenges with revelation from God's Word is what really matters. If you know how to minister to yourself, you can minister in your car, at your house or wherever you are when you need to receive something from God. But if all you know how to do is chase after preachers who flow in the gifts of the Spirit, then you will be in a bind if you are by yourself and need to call on God without their help!

You can't always call Brother or Sister so-and-so to come minister to you. But you can always call on God and receive whatever it is you need if you have revelation knowledge from the Word of God. If a situation came up suddenly, you could minister on the spot. That's why I said that signs come and go, but revelation always remains the same. Revelation supersedes signs. The Church has allowed *signs* to supersede *revelation,* and many have been whipped and defeated in life as a result.

We read Matthew 16:1-11. Now let's get to the nitty-gritty of the importance of revelation knowledge.

> **When Jesus came into the coasts of Caesarea Philippi,**
> **he asked his disciples, saying, Whom do men say that I the**
> **Son of man am?**
>
> MATTHEW 16:13

Now, as I said, the disciples had been with Jesus, but they did not really know Him. One reason they did not know Him is that they were dealing with signs instead of revelation. Jesus had constantly revealed Himself, and every time He did, He showed forth a greater revelation of the Father God. But when it came right down to it, the disciples didn't really know who Jesus was.

## WHO DO *YOU* SAY JESUS IS?

Notice Jesus asked them, ...**Whom do men say that I the Son of man am?** Look at some of the things they said.

> **And they said, Some say that thou art John the Baptist:**
> **some, Elias; and others, Jeremias, or one of the prophets.**
>
> MATTHEW 16:14

Jesus finally got the right answer from Peter, who said, **Thou art the Christ, the Son of the living God** (v. 16).

Notice, when the disciples answered Jesus, SOME **say that thou art John the Baptist: some, Elias; and others, Jeremias, or one of the prophets** (v. 14), Jesus came back and asked, **But whom say YE that I am?** (v. 15).

You see, you cannot personally know Jesus without a revelation—without eyes to see, ears to hear and a heart to understand. And you cannot recognize when Jesus and the Spirit of God are moving in your midst without a revelation of who Jesus is. In other words, the only way you are going to be a good sheep in the flock is to understand who your leader is. And you have to have a revelation of it—you can't go by fleshly signs. You have to have a revelation in your spirit.

Some people are content to follow signs. But you can't grow to maturity and be full-blast, 100 percent for God without a revelation. If you only know "what's what" spiritually because someone else told you so, you don't have a revelation for yourself. You can't simply go by what others say. To be successful in life, you have to go by what you know for yourself.

## THE IMPORTANCE OF REVELATION IN RELATIONSHIPS

When I hold marriage workshops, I tell husbands and wives not to listen to what others say about their spouses. They know their spouses better than anybody else. They know them intimately, in their hearts as well as in their minds. So why should they bother about what someone else tells them about their mates?

I know my wife! Why? Because I have eyes that see and ears that hear. My eyes see further than walls or buildings or even the miles that sometimes separate us. And she has eyes to see and ears to hear too. The Lord will tell her things about me, so I want everything He tells her to be good, not bad!

## LIVING CLOSE TO GOD—THE PRICE OF REVELATION

Someone might say, "Well, I don't want that kind of revelation of God and Jesus. I just don't want to live that close." Well, you can't live in the full blessings and the full power of God if you don't want to live close in fellowship with Him.

I want to share something else from that passage in Matthew 16.

**And Simon Peter answered and said, Thou art the Christ, the Son of the living God.**

**And Jesus answered and said unto him, Blessed art thou, Simon Barjona: for flesh and blood hath not revealed it unto thee, but my Father which is in heaven.**

MATTHEW 16:16,17

What was Jesus saying to Peter in verse 17? He was saying, in effect, "You are blessed, for you have eyes that can see, ears that can hear and a heart than can understand. And you are converted. I can work with you. I can give you anything you need or want."

As I said before, Peter's natural eyes, ears and heart did not reveal to him the answer that Jesus was the Christ, the Son of the living God. It was Peter's *spirit* that revealed it to him. And God will reveal things to your spirit too. He does it through His Word and through His Spirit. He gives you the ability to understand situations from His point of view and to have your situations converted to your good and His glory. He lives inside of you if you are a Christian. And that force of the power of God and the revelation of who Jesus is, are more powerful than any force, situation, circumstance or obstacle that's on the outside. That force will help you convert your *contests* into *conquests!*

# Chapter 7

## Faith Fight *or Faith* Failure?

*For I am not ashamed of the gospel of Christ:*
*for it is the power of God unto salvation to every one*
*that believeth; to the Jew first, and also to the Greek.*
*For therein is the righteousness of God revealed from*
*faith to faith: as it is written, The just shall live by faith.*

—ROMANS 1:16,17

Notice the phrase in verse 17, **For therein is the righteousness of God revealed FROM FAITH TO FAITH....** Then notice the last part of that verse: ...**The just shall LIVE by faith.** Those two statements are just another testimony to the fact that the faith fight is a continual fight. Certainly, there are endings to certain situations you may deal with—certain faith projects. But it says that the just shall *live* by faith. In other words, faith is a lifestyle.

You begin certain projects in faith and maintain a certain stand in faith when you are challenged by life's circumstances. But you have to *continue* in faith for God to finish the job for you. The same steps whereby you were saved are the steps you take in every faith project you deal with. You believe in your heart, and you confess that Word that is in your heart. God will always back up His Word and do whatever you need Him to do when you take a stand in faith and *continue* in faith.

The devil will try to get you to give up on the faith fight. He will try to get you to give up and quit before your faith fight is finished— before you get your answer. Do not listen to the voice of the enemy. He has a voice, and he will talk to you. He'll try to talk you out of your faith.

Has the voice of the enemy ever spoken to you when you were facing some challenge and you were dealing with it in faith? Has he ever said something to you, such as, "What are you going to do now? You've got to do something. What are you going to do?"

## Go to Bed, Get Up and Praise the Lord!

I'll tell you what to do when the enemy comes with his lies. The answer is found in Mark 4.

> **And he [Jesus] said, So is the kingdom of God, as if a man should cast seed into the ground; And should sleep, and rise night and day, and the seed should spring and grow up, he knoweth not how. For the earth bringeth forth fruit of herself; first the blade, then the ear, after that the full corn in the ear.**
>
> MARK 4:26-28

You see, when you cast the seed of the Word in the ground, you don't know exactly *how* that seed grows—you just know that it grows. And you sleep and rise night and day, expecting that seed to grow and sprout. So what should you do when the enemy comes with his lies to try to get you to pull your faith seed out of the ground? You should just go to bed, get up and praise the Lord!

In other words, just go about your business, praising the Lord and expecting the answer to come. The devil and demons will not like that. Demons will say about a person who goes to bed, gets up and praises the Lord, "That Christian must be crazy! Doesn't he know what we're trying to do to him? He's stupid. Doesn't he know we're trying to mess him up?" Those demons will call a hot line to hell and say to the devil, "Look, we do not want this assignment. All this Christian is doing at his house is going to bed, getting up and praising the Lord. He is driving us crazy! We want to tear his house up, but we cannot."

You see, the devil wants to get you to grumble, gripe, cry and complain. He doesn't want you to go to bed, get up and praise the Lord that your faith is working—that the seed of the Word of God is growing and producing results for you.

Let's read what the gospel of John has to say about the voice of the "stranger," the devil.

> **Verily, verily, I [Jesus] say unto you, He that entereth not by the door into the sheepfold, but climbeth up some other way, the same is a thief and a robber. But he that entereth in by the door is the shepherd of the sheep. To him the porter openeth; and the sheep hear his voice: and he calleth his own sheep by name, and leadeth them out. And when he putteth forth his own sheep, he goeth before them, and the sheep follow him: for they know his voice. And a stranger will they not follow, but will flee from him: for they know not the voice of strangers.**
>
> JOHN 10:1-5

First, notice that it says in verse 4, **For they** [the sheep] **know his** [Jesus'] **voice.** That is a good verse to underline in your Bible as well as to confess: "I know the voice of Jesus, my Shepherd."

Also notice something in verse 3: **The sheep hear his voice: and he calleth his own sheep by name, and leadeth them out.** You see, when you are dealing with something in faith, seeking God, He will call you by your name, and He will lead you out!

Now look at verses 4 and 5 again: **For they know his voice. And a stranger will they not follow, but will flee from him: for they know not the voice of strangers.** These verses do not mean that the sheep will "know not" when a strange voice is talking to them. It means that they are not *hooked up* with the voice of strangers; they are hooked up with the voice of the Good Shepherd.

## LISTENING TO THE VOICE OF THE ENEMY CAN COST YOU

The enemy's voice is the voice of a stranger. So when he begins to tell you what he is going to do, don't pay any attention to him, because his voice is not the voice of the Good Shepherd—the voice of the Lord. If you are going to deal properly with challenges of life, you can't afford to listen to the voice of the enemy. He will talk you out of your faith and your victory if you do.

**There are, it may be, so many kinds of voices in the world, and none of them is without signification.**

**1 CORINTHIANS 14:10**

There are a whole lot of voices out there in the world. But if you learn that one voice, the voice of your Shepherd, you will recognize when a different voice is calling to you. For example, I know my wife's voice. Other women could call my house, pretending to be my wife, but the minute I heard any other woman speak, I would know that it wasn't my wife because I know my wife's voice. I've been listening to her beautiful voice for more than twenty-two years, and I *know* it! I could single her voice out over 10,000 others.

So once you single out a voice, other voices don't bother you. In the Church today, there are many different voices. There are voices of religion, tradition, philosophy, prejudice and the doctrines of men. But, you see, once believers single out the truth, those other voices will stand out as false, unable to have any effect on them.

First Corinthians 14:10 says, **There are...many kinds of voices in the world, and none of them is without signification** [or meaning]. In other words, none of these voices in the world is without meaning. Those voices mean something. So if you listen to the wrong one, you are going to get whatever it means. If you listen to it long enough, whatever that voice means is going to be accomplished in your life.

It is important to listen to what God has said and not to what the devil and the world say.

**Let your conversation be without covetousness; and be content with such things as ye have: for HE [the Lord] hath SAID, I will never leave thee, nor forsake thee. So that we may boldly SAY, The Lord is my helper, and I will not fear what man shall do unto me.**

HEBREWS 13:5,6

Look at that phrase in verse 5 ...FOR HE HATH SAID.... If you are listening to the Lord's voice, and the enemy tries to tell you something, you won't pay any attention to the enemy, **for He** [the Lord] **hath said** something different! You'll know what *He,* the Lord, has said, and that will be good enough for you.

So, looking at Hebrews 13, let's see what He has said: **I will never leave thee, nor forsake thee.** This verse is the voice of the Father and of the Good Shepherd. So when the enemy comes along, this verse will help you discern the enemy's voice so that you won't follow it. If he says, "You're going through something, and the Lord is not with you. You are all by yourself, and I am going to whip you," you should know that is the voice of a stranger, because *God* has said, "I will *never* leave you nor forsake you." You can say, "No, Mr. Devil, you are a liar, because I know the voice of my Shepherd. He is speaking to me in Hebrews 13:5 and 6. Haven't you ever read those verses? Here, let me read them to you."

## GOD IS FAITHFUL, ESPECIALLY IN THE "TIGHT SPOTS"

The enemy will try to talk to you. He will try to talk you out of your faith, especially in the tight spots. Have you ever been in a tight spot? Of course you have. We are all going to go through some tight spots in life, because we can't *grow* until we *know* for ourselves the voice of the Shepherd and the fact that He is faithful to deliver us out of any situation or circumstance.

There are times when tests and trials will come your way, and you will have to regroup and get on the stick, so to speak, with your faith. You might find yourself in the dust, saying, "What am I doing down here with the devil, listening to his lies?" Just dust yourself off and get back where you are supposed to be. You might have to jump up and holler, "No, devil! I'm not going to be defeated!"

## REFUSE TO TOLERATE DEFEAT

There have been times when I've been enjoying the Lord and enjoying life when, all of a sudden, the devil would come to me, telling me all kinds of stuff he was going to do. I would jump up and holler, "Who are you talking to? What do you mean by that? How did you get on this property, anyway?" and I'd just take authority over him out loud. I will not tolerate the devil and defeat.

How can I be that bold? I can't listen to the devil when I know that God has said, **I will never leave thee nor forsake thee.** I have a question for you. How long is "never"? I mean, maybe you're going through a challenge, and you're acting as if you have lived beyond the point of "never"—as if God has left you! But He hasn't left you, and He never will.

The next time you begin murmuring and complaining about life, you need to remember that you are not beyond "never." You can't reach the point in life beyond "never" where the Lord has forsaken you. The next time you catch yourself complaining, you ought to say to yourself, "I'm acting as if I'm beyond never." Or if you hear your spouse complaining and saying, "I just don't know how we're going to make it," you need to say, "Honey, you're acting as if you just moved beyond never."

Do you believe that the Lord is with you? Do you believe there is any possible way for you to go down in defeat when the Lord is with you? You are going to have many opportunities in life to answer these questions. The correct answer is, "No way." That word "never" in Hebrews 13:5 means *never!*

I really like the part that says, **I will never...forsake thee,** because that means He will fight for you when the time comes to fight. It means He will not turn cold on you. It means He is going to stay there until you win! One of the Old Testament writers said, **The battle is not yours, but God's** (2 Chronicles 20:15). Really, what happens in the good fight of faith when you live and act properly according to the Word is that you do not actually have to fight. The only fight you have to fight is the faith fight—laboring to enter into and to *stay* in faith. The actual battle is the Lord's. He will fight it for you and win!

## THE FAITH LIFE IS NOT A STRUGGLE

You see, God has to back up your faith, or He is not God. People have tried to make the faith walk hard. But this life of faith and abundance and of walking with God is not a hard life. The voice of the enemy has lied to the Church and has told us it is hard—that we can only have a measure of success in life. Then the devil has told us that in order for us to have success, we have to struggle with this program and that program, trying to make something work in our flesh—in ourselves.

We thought we had to go to church three times on Sunday to make things work, and we've had folks changing clothes all day, going back and forth to church. They were so busy, they didn't have time to kiss their children or to take a Sunday afternoon drive with their families. People are going to church—church here, church there; church in the morning, church in the evening, church at supper time. And they are still defeated!

## THERE IS NO SUBSTITUTE FOR THE WORD

Why are Christians sometimes defeated? Because it does not make any difference how many times you go into a church *building*—if you are not getting the Word of God, the devil is still going to whip your behind! You could go to church every day if you wanted to, but if you are not in the Word of God, the devil is going to meet you on Monday morning, slap you "upside the head," take your lunch bucket and tell you that you are going to have a terrible day and that you are not going to be able to do anything about it! Then when you come home, he is going to start some mess at your house. And you won't be able to stop him, because you will have been working on getting inside a church building instead of getting the Word of God inside of *you!*

The Word of God says, **I will never leave thee nor forsake thee.** You are not forsaken, because you are "attached." You are one with the Father (John 17:11,21,22). You are not forsaken just because a big Goliath comes across your path, hollering at you. God is with you, so just get out your slingshot!

114

## THERE IS NO PLACE FOR SELF-PITY IN THE FAITH LIFE

Some people feel forsaken by God, and they start feeling sorry for themselves. That is not the time to feel sorry for yourself. Get off that sympathy trail, because that's the devil's trail, and get on the "hallelujah" trail where the Lord is! He will never leave you nor forsake you!

Hebrews 13:6 tells us what God wants us to do about the tests and trials of life, knowing that He will never leave us nor forsake us.

**So that we may boldly say, The Lord is my helper, and I will not fear what man shall do unto me.**

HEBREWS 13:6

When challenges come God wants us to boldly say, "The Lord is my helper. I will not fear." He wants us to say to the devil, "That's not good enough to get me off my faith, devil. I'm with the Lord. You'd better leave me alone."

## GOD WANTS US TO HAVE BOLD FAITH

Notice it said, **That we may BOLDLY say, The Lord is my helper.** God wants us to be bold. He wants us to knock on hell's door and say, "Hey, you devil and demons, the Lord is my helper!" Don't let the devil knock on *your* door; you go knock on *his* door!

Some morning after you have fellowshipped with and praised the Lord, you ought to knock on the devil's door and say, "What do you have on your mind? I tell you right now, nothing is going to happen to me. I'm not going to have any accident. I'm not going to be sick. You are not going to rob me of my finances. Nothing is going to break down today. I just stopped by to tell you that I'm going to have a good day, in the Name of Jesus!"

Most people wait for the devil to knock on their doors first. They never wake the devil up; they always let him wake *them* up. But when you are bold and full of the knowledge of God's Word, you will make some announcements to the devil. You will say, "As for me and my house, we are going to serve the Lord" (Joshua 24:15)!

Sometimes it's better to get up and tell the devil something than to just sit back and wait for him to speak to you. That way you won't have to listen to him all day. When you are finished making your announcements to the devil, tell him, "I'm not going to listen to anything you say today."

Some people are afraid to do that. They just want to act "nice." They'll say, "I'm not going to do all that stuff that preacher is saying. I'm just going to act nice. I'm going to pray and be quiet." But the devil will come after you anyway, whether you act nice or not, because he is the god of this world (2 Corinthians 4:4). So you might as well be bold and "hit" him first!

Growing up, I was taught by my older brothers to always hit first. They said if someone tried to pick a fight with me, and I knew he was going to hit me sooner or later, to just hit him first. They said, "Whether you can whip him or not, hit him!"

You know, you can't be a little "worm" of a Christian and expect to get the devil out of your face. The Bible says to *resist* the devil, and he will flee from you (James 4:7). You have to say to the devil, "Look, get back from me. Move on in the Name of Jesus!" And he will flee from you.

The Lord has said too many good things to us in His Word and has given us too much authority over the devil for us to be listening to the voice of the enemy. God's Word is good enough! Let's look at a Scripture in Numbers 23 that illustrates that fact.

**God is not a man, that he should lie; neither the son of man, that he should repent: hath he said, and shall he not do it? or hath he spoken, and shall he not make it good?**

NUMBERS 23:19

I love that verse! He *will* make it good. So do not listen to the voice of the enemy. Do not entertain the thoughts of the enemy. And do not repeat the words of the enemy. Do not say what he says. Remember, you will have in this life what you say (Mark 11:23). So say what you desire, not what the devil says he's going to do to you.

## WHAT IS HINDERING YOU?

As I already said, there are challenges to this Christian walk. You can either fight the good fight of faith, or you can have a faith failure. The world is full of faith failures. The world is full of defeated Christians who have the ability in them to be world overcomers and conquerors. They have the potential to reign as kings in life in Christ Jesus (Romans 5:17). But because of religion, tradition, philosophy, prejudice, the doctrines of men and a whole lot of other junk, they have not been able to stand their ground. They have been listening to the wrong voices.

Some Christians don't have the respect for the things of God that they used to have. One reason for that is that many ministers do not have the anointing on their lives as they should so that people could experience God in demonstration and, therefore, have reverence for Him. You could mention the word "church" to some sinners, and they will break out and laugh. Many things that go on in the Name of the Lord are nothing more than "carnival showmanship." They have no real power or anointing.

In fact, many Christians are just waiting to go to heaven. They're waiting at the "bus stop" to catch the heaven bus! Certainly, we're supposed to look forward to heaven, but there are some things the Father God wants for us here on the earth. He wants us to be well—healed and whole. He wants our needs to be met. He wants us to represent Him well on this planet earth, operating and functioning in His power.

## YOU CANNOT FIGHT IGNORANTLY AND WIN

But you cannot do it ignorantly. You cannot operate in God's power if you do not know how to fight the good fight of faith. Without certain knowledge, you won't put up a fight when challenges confront you.

I tell you, I am tired of seeing faith failures in the Church. I am tired of seeing people in the Church in the welfare line. I am tired of hearing people say, "I don't know how I'm going to make it." That should not be! We serve an awesome, dynamic God! And He is concerned about our everyday affairs.

Now, if you are going to live in the winning circle, you have no choice—you must fight the good fight of faith, and you must fight it until you win. You cannot decide, "Well, I don't believe I want to fight the good fight of faith. I believe I'm just going to be a church member. I am just going to pay my dues and be a good church member. I'm sure the Lord will take care of me." With that attitude, you are going to get whipped from the top of your head to the bottom of your feet! The Lord has done His part. Now you have to do your part.

As I said, the Church has had many faith failures. The reason is not so much that our faith has failed, but that we have failed to properly *use* our faith.

Let me show you an example in the gospel of Luke in which someone had an opportunity to either fight or fail.

**And the Lord said, Simon, Simon [talking about Peter],
behold, Satan hath desired to have you, that he may sift you
as wheat.**

LUKE 22:31

Jesus told Peter that Satan desired to have him. But let me tell
you right now—Satan desires to have you too. He desires to have
your marriage, your job, your health and your prosperity. He will try
to take control of you through alcohol, dope, ungodly living and
wrong thinking. He doesn't mind the fact that you're a church
member. He doesn't even mind it if you sing in the choir—as long as
he can have you once you leave that church service.

——— YOU HAVE A CHOICE—DON'T ALLOW ———<br>SATAN TO HAVE YOU!

But just because Satan *desires* to have you doesn't mean he is
automatically going to have you! He can't just automatically steal,
kill and destroy. But the only way to keep him from having you is to
fight the good fight of faith.

Someone may ask, "Well, what does he want to do with me once
he has me?" Luke 22:31 tells us: ...**that he may sift you as wheat.**

What does that word "sift" mean? It means *to scatter.*[1] Satan
desires to scatter you around so that you just live a haphazard life,
never having any direction and never having any victory. When you
are "scattered around," you are unstable—sometimes up and
sometimes down—and you have no firm conviction, no firm direction and no firm revelation of God and His Word. Satan desires to sift
you to the point that you do not know what tomorrow will bring. He
wants to scatter you and make you sick, broke and confused.

I could take you to churches today and show you Christians who
are as scattered as they can be. I mean, they are gossiping all day

119

long. You can't talk to them fifteen minutes without their bringing up fifteen other people to talk against. Some Christians are still cursing, just living shameful lives. They are scattered. Their faith is failing in certain areas.

You've got to have faith not to sin. Some people say, "Well, I don't need faith to live free from sin. I can take what comes to me in life without sinning." Child, your flesh can't take *anything!* You need some *faith* not to sin!

## Your Faith Is Your Shield Against Failure

If your *faith* does not fail, *you* will not fail. Let's look at another part of Luke 22:32. After Jesus said, **I have prayed for thee, that thy faith fail not...**, He said, **...and when thou art converted, strengthen thy brethren.** We already talked about that word "converted" from the standpoint of converting contests to conquests—of converting the natural to the supernatural.

The first thing that comes to mind when reading that word "converted" is spiritual conversion or being born again. But, really, Peter was not even at the point of being born again, because nobody in Matthew, Mark, Luke or John was born again. They could not be New Testament Christians until Jesus Christ died, rose again and sat down at the right hand of the Most High.

Jesus was the first-born. When He died, rose again and ascended to the Father, then all of us who accepted Jesus could come into the family of God. So in Luke 22:32, the word "converted" was not talking about Peter's conversion of being born again. It was talking about a situation being converted, or turned around, in his life—converted from a faith *failure* to a faith *fight.*

*In life, we are either going to fight the faith fight, or we are going to have a faith failure!*

120

Satan desires to have us. But, I tell you, I have made up my mind that he is not going to have me! I belong to Somebody else. I am private property—God's property!

How about you? Have you made up your mind?

## "I HAVE PRAYED FOR YOU— THAT YOUR FAITH FAIL NOT!"

So we know that Satan desires to have us that he may sift us or scatter us around as wheat. Jesus told us that in Luke 22:31. But look at what Jesus said in the next verse.

> **But I have prayed for thee, that thy faith fail not: and when thou art converted, strengthen thy brethren.**
>
> LUKE 22:32

Jesus was telling Peter, "Satan has desired to have you. But I have prayed for you." Why did Jesus pray for Peter? For one reason: *that his faith fail not!* Just think of all the other things you or I might think Jesus should have prayed for. But there are not "fourteen steps to keep Satan from scattering you"! No, there's only *one* thing—fighting the good fight of faith—and that one thing will activate everything else you need to withstand Satan.

Can you see that? In other words, Jesus was saying that Satan desires to have you so he can scatter you. But if your faith is standing, he cannot do it. If you do not have a faith failure, you will be able to fight the good fight of faith. You will be able to lay hold on eternal life and finish your course in victory.

Why didn't Jesus pray for Peter that his *love* fail not? Why didn't He pray that his *forgiveness* would fail not? Do you see how important it is not to have a faith failure?

121

If you are honest, you would probably admit that at some point in your Christian life, Satan has scattered you. I know in my own life, there were times he had me scattered. I didn't know whether I was coming or going! I didn't know how to deal with the devil by faith.

## WE DON'T HAVE TO BE SCATTERED IN OUR FAITH

When you are in a position where you are scattered in your faith, just settle down with God, meditate on His Word and then stick with the Word. Revelation will come. Your heart will come to understand what the will of the Lord is, and neither the devil nor anybody else will be able to stop you.

When Jesus told Peter that Satan desired to have him so that he could sift him, Jesus used wheat as an illustration. He said, ...**Satan hath desired to have you, that he may sift you as** WHEAT. You know, wheat cannot resist scattering. Wheat has no life in itself, so man can just take it and scatter it. But in the faith fight, we are not as wheat, and we can resist the devil. Too many Christians have been *receiving* from the devil when they should have been *resisting* him.

## HOW TO RESIST THE SCATTERER

Recently, I got up to preach to my congregation, and my voice was giving out on me; I could hardly talk. The people could barely understand what I was saying. But I was standing my ground in faith. I taught for nearly an hour and never said anything about it to the people. I just kept teaching as if nothing were wrong, because I had already used my faith against that condition. Later on, I was talking clearly again as if I'd never been sick, because I knew how to resist the devil.

Let's look at a familiar verse in James 4 about resisting the devil.

**Submit yourselves therefore to God. Resist the devil, and he will flee from you.**

JAMES 4:7

First, we read that Jesus told Peter that Satan desired to sift him as wheat. Then in this verse, the Lord is saying to resist the devil, and he will flee from you. Well, how are we going to resist the devil? Certainly, the first part of that verse gives us a clue: **Submit yourselves therefore to God....** But there is something specific that gives us the ability to resist the devil: *faith.*

**Whom [the devil] resist stedfast in the FAITH, knowing that the same afflictions are accomplished in your brethren that are in the world.**

1 PETER 5:9

So, certainly, you resist the devil by giving him no place, by pleading the blood of Jesus and by speaking the Word. But you could plead the blood and speak the Word and go through all kinds of motions—yet if you did not have faith, the devil would not move!

Let's look at First Peter 5:9 in its context.

**Humble yourselves therefore under the mighty hand of God, that he may exalt you in due time: Casting all your care upon him; for he careth for you. Be sober, be vigilant; because your adversary the devil, as a roaring lion, walketh about, seeking whom he may devour: Whom resist stedfast in the faith, knowing that the same afflictions are accomplished in your brethren that are in the world. But the God of all grace, who hath called us unto his eternal glory by Christ Jesus, after that ye have suffered a while, make you perfect, stablish, strengthen, settle you.**

1 PETER 5:6-10

Look at verse 7 in *The Amplified Bible:* **Casting the whole of your care [all your anxieties, all your worries, all your concerns, once and for all] on Him, for He cares for you affectionately, and cares about you watchfully.** I'm still talking about faith. It takes faith to cast your cares on the Lord. I mean, when hell is hounding you and is on your trail with things hitting you left and right, you aren't going to be able to cast your cares on the Lord in the flesh. No, you're going to have to do it in the Spirit. You can't cast your cares on the Lord by being a crybaby and saying, "Oh, Lord, I'm hurting." No, you cast your cares on the Lord by faith and, specifically, by humbling yourself under the mighty hand of God!

> **Humble yourselves therefore under the mighty hand of God....** CASTING ALL YOUR CARE **upon him; for he careth for you.**
>
> 1 PETER 5:6,7

Why do you have to cast your cares on the Lord by faith? Because if you are sitting down with a pile of cares in your lap, you are going to have to cast them off on the Lord and *keep* them cast on Him long enough for Him to take care of them and do something about them for you. That takes faith. Also, you have to cast those cares by faith, because it is faith that changes the natural facts, or circumstances, into *faith* facts. Remember, it is faith that converts your contests into conquests and takes your circumstances from the natural realm to the realm of the supernatural. Or we could say it like this: It is faith that causes the Spirit realm to kick in on your behalf. And the Spirit realm is greater than the natural realm. The Spirit realm has the ability to bring to realization the thing that you are believing God for.

So, you see, you've got to live by faith, cast your cares on the Lord by faith and resist the devil by faith. You can't go by your natural feelings. And you need to stop trying to figure things out. Often, when you think about problems and circumstances and try to figure them out in your mind, you will get them in more of a jumble than they were before. And if you allow yourself to get caught up in the cares and affairs of life, you won't be at peace and at rest and you won't have any energy to seek first the Kingdom of God.

## GOD WANTS YOU TO BE CAREFREE!

So we know that we're supposed to cast our cares on the Lord. Actually, that verse says, **Casting ALL your care upon him; for he careth for you.** How many cares? *All of them.*

So if you cast *all* your cares on the Lord by faith, how many cares would you have left? None! God wants us to cast all of our cares on Him so we can sleep well, eat well and *live* well! But being full of worries and cares will mess you up spiritually. It will hinder you from resisting the devil.

The next verse in First Peter 5 implies this.

> **Be sober, be vigilant; because your adversary the devil, as a roaring lion, walketh about, seeking whom he may devour.**
>
> 1 PETER 5:8

Notice, the devil walks about, seeking. The devil has to look for somebody to devour. He can't just devour any Christian. He knows he cannot randomly run through a church and make just anybody do anything he wants him to do. Why? Because there are some who are going to have their shields of faith up when he tries to make a run on them. They will have on that breastplate of righteousness. They will have their loins girded about with truth. (See Ephesians 6:13-17.)

So the devil goes around saying, "Who can I find to cause disturbance and trouble in their lives?" But when he sees that shield of faith, he says, "I believe I'll go somewhere else." You see, the devil cannot just do anything he wants to do. We have made the devil out to be too big. The Bible says, "He goes about seeking whom he *may* devour." Well, speaking for myself, he "may *not*" devour me! I am going to serve God. I am going to give God first place in my life, and I am going to walk by faith and fight the good fight of faith when challenges arise.

I have made up my mind that I'm going to obey God and do whatever the Spirit of God tells me to do. I do not care what man says. I do not care what *anybody* says. And I'm going to be blessed coming in and going out as a result. The devil is not going to have me. You can go home and make friends with him and think he is your buddy if you want to. But he is going to end up whipping you here on earth and carrying you to hell if you don't straighten up!

## THE PLEASURE OF SIN IS ONLY FOR A SEASON

The Bible talks about **the pleasures of sin for a season** (Hebrews 11:25). You can have temporary things if you want—pleasures and even material possessions—by getting in "tight" with the devil. But those things are not going to last. I've heard sinners talking about their empires—the kinds of houses they live in and the kinds of cars they drive. But how long are they going to be able to hold on to those things? The Bible says that the evildoer shall be cut off (Psalms 37:9). There aren't going to be any more pleasures in hell—just a lot of screaming.

Now, I do not talk about hell a whole lot, because I am not going there. But hell is a real place. And there are some people there now who are screaming, "Oh, if only I had paid attention when the altar call was made! If only I had gone forward and accepted Jesus as my Savior! But it's too late!"

Not only is hell real, but hell on earth is real too. Some people have hell on earth because they do not have the Word of God. Others *catch* hell on earth because they have learned a little something about

126

operating in the things of God. The devil tries to give them hell. And *people* try to give them hell by persecuting them. But all of that can be conquered and overcome. How? By staying in the faith fight!

## GOD WANTS US TO BE INFORMED, NOT IGNORANT

I always tell my congregation that they'd better appreciate having a good church to attend! I'm not lifting myself up or bragging on my own strengths. I'm bragging on the Word of God that is lifted up in my church and preached and taught. Some people don't have a good church, and they never get any victory over the hell in their lives. There are church people all over this country who exit their church doors every Sunday just as ignorant as they can be about spiritual things.

I get tired of seeing Christians just "slouching" in life. They say, "I belong to the Lord," and, certainly, they do. But they don't know anything. They are ignorant; and that hurts me, because I know I could put something in them. They talk about how they know the Lord, but the devil is whipping them in life.

God does not want us to be ignorant. That's why He has given us His Word. We are told in James 4 to submit to God and to resist the devil. But I believe that Peter opened it up even more clearly to us in First Peter 5. James told us to resist the devil (James 4:7). Peter told us to resist him steadfastly **in the faith** (1 Peter 5:9).

Now, James 4:7 is good and right. We are supposed to submit to God and resist the devil. But we must have the revelation of how to do it. We submit ourselves to God *by faith.* We resist the devil *by faith.* For example, if your body is racked with pain, you cannot resist the devil by *feelings.* You have to resist him by *faith.* Certainly, you cannot deny the fact that your body is hurting, because in the natural, it *is* hurting! If you have a tumor in your body, you cannot deny its existence and say it's not there. But you *can* resist it. You can tell it that it does not have the right to exist in your body. You can tell that tumor to pack its bags and get out, in Jesus' Name!

So, you see, you have to resist the devil in faith. I mean, when the devil is really after you, you have to resist him, and you have to know what you are doing. You can't just sit back and receive from him what he wants to do to you. I tell you, the devil will try to knock you down, stomp you in the ground and bury you alive. And he uses the sense realm to do it. In other words, every one of your senses may tell you that your faith is not working, that you're going under, that you're not going to make it this time. But you can take the Word of God, the sword of the Spirit, and look that devil straight in the eyes, and say, "Devil, in the Name of Jesus, I *resist* you!"

## SPIRITUAL PERSISTENCE ALWAYS PAYS

I have had moments in which the devil has tried to put some kind of symptom on me, and I have said, "No! I resist you, in Jesus' Name"; and, *whoosh,* the symptom would be gone! Now, there are some persistent demons who will try to stay awhile. So you need to learn how to fight the good fight of faith and stand your ground so you'll know how to deal with the persistent ones. If you do not know how to deal with the persistent ones, you are not going to be able to deal with the little flaky ones. You will just quit, give up and cave in at the first sign of opposition.

If you go into a test or trial, and it seems as if things are not getting any better after you've used your faith, you are dealing with some persistent devils. So *you* have to learn how to be persistent too. You have to be steadfast in the faith. You have to look those demons straight on and tell them, "I am under the blood, and I am going to stand my ground. I am on holy ground, and I shall not be moved."

Someone may ask, "Well, how long do I stand my ground?" Until you win!

God cannot do anything for you unless you are doing your part according to the Word. Since He said we are to resist the devil steadfast in the faith, then we'd better know as much as we can about this business of faith.

Look at Mark 9.

> And one of the multitude answered and said, Master, I have brought unto thee my son, which hath a dumb spirit; And wheresoever he taketh him, he teareth him: and he foameth, and gnasheth with his teeth, and pineth away: and I spake to thy disciples that they should cast him out; and they could not. He answereth him, and saith, O faithless generation, how long shall I be with you? how long shall I suffer you? bring him unto me. And they brought him unto him: and when he saw him, straightway the spirit tare him; and he fell on the ground, and wallowed foaming. And he asked his father, How long is it ago since this came unto him? And he said, Of a child. And ofttimes it hath cast him into the fire, and into the waters, to destroy him: but if thou canst do any thing, have compassion on us, and help us. Jesus said unto him, If thou canst believe, all things are possible to him that believeth. And straightway the father of the child cried out, and said with tears, Lord, I believe; help thou mine unbelief.
>
> MARK 9:17-24

This man had brought his son to the disciples to try to get some help for him. Then the disciples brought the boy to Jesus. The father said to Jesus, **If thou canst do any thing, have compassion on us, and help us** (v. 22). Then notice how Jesus answered the man: **If thou canst believe, all things are possible to him that believeth** (v. 23).

You see, the issue here was not whether or not the Lord could help the man. The issue was whether the man could cooperate with the Lord in faith. Jesus said, "All things are possible." In other words, Jesus was saying, "I can do it." But the first part of that verse says, IF THOU CANST BELIEVE, **all things are possible to him that** BELIEVETH.

Think about your own case now. What are you going through? Ask yourself, "How many things did Jesus say were possible to him who believes?" *All* things are possible!

In Mark 9, when Jesus said to the boy's father, "All things are possible to him that believes," that father cried out, **Lord, I believe; help thou mine unbelief** (v. 24). Actually, the Lord cannot help your unbelief. He can point you to His Word, but you are going to have to help your own unbelief.

God has given us the means in His Word to have all the faith we need to receive whatever it is we desire. So God does not help *unbelief;* He helps the *believer!*

If someone were sitting in a dead, dry church, crying, "Lord, help my unbelief," the Lord would probably tell him to get up out of that unbelieving church! So, you see, it is up to us to do something about our unbelief. The responsibility lies with us to believe God and what He has said in His Word.

Let me show you another verse that will illustrate this fact to you more clearly. It's found in Mark 5.

**And when Jesus was passed over again by ship unto the other side, much people gathered unto him: and he was nigh unto the sea. And, behold, there cometh one of the rulers of the synagogue, Jairus by name; and when he saw him, he fell at his feet, And besought him greatly, saying, My little daughter lieth at the point of death: I pray thee, come and lay thy hands on her, that she may be healed; and**

130

she shall live. And Jesus went with him; and much people followed him, and thronged him.

While he yet spake, there came from the ruler of the synagogue's house certain which said, Thy daughter is dead: why troublest thou the Master any further? As soon as Jesus heard the word that was spoken, he saith unto the ruler of the synagogue, Be not afraid, only believe.

MARK 5:21-24,35,36

Now, on His way to heal Jairus' daughter, Jesus was stopped by the woman with the issue of blood.

And Jesus went with him; and much people followed him, and thronged him. And a certain woman, which had an issue of blood twelve years, And had suffered many things of many physicians, and had spent all that she had, and was nothing bettered, but rather grew worse, When she had heard of Jesus, came in the press behind, and touched his garment. For she said, If I may touch but his clothes, I shall be whole. And straightway the fountain of her blood was dried up; and she felt in her body that she was healed of that plague.

And he said unto her, Daughter, thy faith hath made thee whole; go in peace, and be whole of thy plague.

MARK 5:24-29,34

Jairus had said to Jesus in verse 23, **My little daughter lieth at the point of death: I pray thee, come and lay thy hands on her, that she may be healed; and she shall live.** Jairus had faith, didn't he?

Now notice what the woman with the issue of blood did: **When she had heard of Jesus, came in the press behind, and touched his garment. For she said, If I may touch but his clothes, I shall be whole** (vv. 27,28).

131

This woman had faith too! And her faith got her what she wanted. Her faith made her whole. But notice what happened after she was healed. While Jesus was still speaking to the woman, Jairus' servants met them, saying, **Thy daughter is dead: why troublest thou the Master any further?** (v. 35). In other words, they were saying, "It's too late. Your daughter died. There is no need to trouble the Master any further."

## FAITH SETS GOD AGAINST YOUR PROBLEM, SO DON'T LET GO OF YOUR FAITH!

Jairus had to make the decision not to let anyone else's faith keep his faith from working for him. In other words, just because the woman with the issue of blood had faith and got her need met, that didn't mean Jairus' faith couldn't get his need met too. The Lord has enough power to go around for everybody!

I tell you, I am not going to let anyone else's faith keep my faith out of God's blessings. Someone else can get all he can, but I'm going to be in there too! I'm going to be "elbowing" right along with that other person, receiving my answer too!

Imagine what Jairus felt when the woman with the issue of blood "interrupted" Jesus! I mean, she slowed Jesus down. But you remember we talked about divine delays. Divine delays are no sign that your faith is not working or that you can't receive what you want from the Lord.

Jairus was undoubtedly thinking, *Who in the world is this woman who stopped Jesus? My daughter is dying. I want to go see about her, and I want Jesus to come with me. We don't have time for this woman with this issue of blood. Who is this, trying to stop the Lord from going to my house?* Jairus could have gotten mad. I mean, he had gotten on his knees and asked the Lord to go heal his daughter. Then here came this woman elbowing her way through the crowd and grabbing hold of Jesus' garment, slowing things down for Jairus.

In fact, I am sure Jairus wanted to cry out, "Lord, You know there is nobody like my little girl! Lord, You're blessing that woman. Why won't You come bless me?" Jairus could have gotten out of faith and said, "Didn't I tell You I wanted You to see about my daughter? What kind of a Savior are You anyway?" But if Jairus would have done that, he would have had a faith failure.

It looked as if Jairus' faith had failed. While Jesus was still tending to the woman with the issue of blood, certain ones came from Jairus' house, saying, "Your daughter just died." Wouldn't that make you mad? But notice what Jesus said the minute He heard that. He turned to Jairus and said, **Be not afraid, only** BELIEVE (v. 36).

You see, those words, "Your daughter is dead," could have caused Jairus' faith to waver. But it was as if Jesus said, "I have to hurry up and say something to him before he opens his mouth." Jairus had heard, "Your daughter is dead." Jesus had to catch Jairus before he opened his mouth and said the same thing: "My daughter is dead." Jairus' faith was already out there, on the line, that his daughter would be healed. He had already said to Jesus, "Come and lay Your hands on her that she might live, and she *shall* live." That was his faith talking, and Jesus did not want him to waver in his faith. He wanted Jairus to hold on to what he had already said. Jesus was saying, "Even though she's already dead, don't say it. I've got the last word."

If we are going to fight the good fight of faith properly and have faith victories instead of faith failures, we are going to have to take God at His Word and learn to hold on to that Word. We are going to have to continue in the faith fight for as long as it takes us to win. Doing this will bring glory to the Father and will move us up into another level of victory in life.

133

# Chapter 8

## How To Maintain an Excellent Spirit in the Midst of Temptation, Part 1

*And Peter calling to remembrance saith unto him [Jesus],*
*Master, behold, the fig tree which thou cursedst is withered away.*
*And Jesus answering saith unto them,*
*Have faith in God [or have God's kind of faith].*
—Mark 11:21,22

In Mark 11, it is made known to us that we can have God's kind of faith. As I said before, the Bible says in several places that the just shall live by faith. It is also made known to us in Hebrews 11:6 that we as believers are to receive from and please the Father by faith.

God wants His children to win in life more than natural parents want their children to win and be successful in life. If you are a parent, not only do you *want* your children to win, but you *purpose* for them to win. You want them to have the best things in life. You want them to have the best education. You want them to take care of their bodies. You want them to esteem spiritual things and to think straight and watch what goes into their minds. You want them to honor and obey you so that it will go well with them all the days of their lives.

The heavenly Father is no different. He wants us to win in life. He wants us to be victorious over all of life's battles. But winning is not automatic just because that is God's will for us. We win over life's challenges by faith. We must, therefore, be students of the Word.

Although God has given us the ability to win, we have to know what to do with what He has given us. We have to be able to push the right buttons and pull the right strings, so to speak, in order to receive the fruition of what the Father has provided for us. We have to arm ourselves with knowledge. We have been plagued by lies in the Church. We have been told to just try to hold on and prove faithful until the end. And we have been told a whole lot of other junk that has kept us from being the type of people that the Father wants us to be.

## Occupy Your Place of Victory

But, thanks be to God, our eyes have been opened, and we have seen things we have never seen before in the Word of God! Now, while we are here on this earth, we are preparing ourselves to occupy. Occupy what? God wants us to "occupy" places of victory. He wants us to "occupy" health. He wants us to "occupy" wealth. He wants us to "occupy" good relationships in our homes, among husbands and wives and families. He wants us to be in dominion. He wants us to dominate the devil and demons. He wants us to control the spirit world by operating in faith and being led by the Spirit, walking in love and having an excellent spirit. That's what I'm going to talk about in this chapter— maintaining an excellent spirit even in the midst of temptation.

## You Were Not Created To Fail

God wants us to win in life, but He did not say we would not have opposition—opponents and opportunities to fail, fall and give up. Those opportunities are present all around us. They are knocking at the door of every person's heart right now. For example, the enemy will say, "You ought to quit. It's no use." But the enemy is a liar. You are a winner. You were born again in the Kingdom of God to win. You were not created to fail.

You might say, "But you don't know my family background. You don't know my last name." I do not need to know it. I know Jesus' last Name—Christ, the Anointed One; the Messiah; the Master! So get up from where you are and dust yourself off. Get ahold of this message so you can learn to fight the good fight of faith with an excellent spirit and win all of life's battles.

As I said in a previous chapter, you are a beneficiary of God's power and blessing. You are a beneficiary of supernatural power in a natural setting. Therefore, your supernatural benefits can change the natural. When problems and pressures come, you can say, "Oh, no, you don't! I am a beneficiary!"

## THE FAITH FIGHT IS NOT A FAIR FIGHT!

You see, a beneficiary should *benefit*. So when the devil tries to fight one of us, it is not even a fair fight. When a person has the Name of Jesus, the blood of Jesus and the sword of the Spirit, which is the Word of God, how can that be a fair fight? The devil does not have any of those things. He cannot use the Name of Jesus. He cannot plead the blood. He cannot use the Word in power. He tries to use it deceptively, but he doesn't have a right to do so. So, you see, it is not even a fair fight. Now, we have been taught that it is not fair to *us* when the devil jumps on us, so to speak. But, really, when we know who we are, what we have and what to do with what we have, we almost want to say, "Poor devil," when he tries to jump on us!

## GUARD THE VAULT OF YOUR SPIRIT

There will be total defeat for the devil in our lives when we really come into agreement with the Father and His Word, occupying our place of victory. To do that, your spirit must become a "vault" for the Word of God to indwell. A vault holds valuable material; and you alone have the combination to unlock the vault of your spirit. The enemy will try to steal the Word, but if you lock it in the vault, he can't steal it. Only you can go in there and take out what you need.

I mean, if something is wrong with your body, do not keep concentrating on what is wrong. Keep looking at what the Word says your body should be. You have the ability to change that circumstance in your body by using the Word of God—by entering the right combination on your vault, pulling out your goods and dressing yourself up with the Word of God.

When confronted with a challenge, you can say, "Wait a minute, Mr. Devil, I've got to go to my vault. I want you to have something. I've got a treasure for you. Stay at the door; I'll be right back." Then run to your vault—get the Word out of your heart—and say, "Here, Mr. Devil. Here's the Word of God, which says, 'By Jesus' stripes I was healed.'" The devil will say, "I don't want that." But you will say, "Well, you've got it anyway. Now get out of here!"

## TWO KEYS

I am going to share with you two things you need to do to successfully fight the faith fight. When you find out what I have to say, you may think that I'm being sacreligious because you may have believed that these two things are unattainable. Maybe you have not fully realized that you are a spirit, you have a soul and you live in a body (1 Thessalonians 5:23) and that you can have the faith of God and the ability to do whatever is necessary to put you over in life's challenges. In the new birth, you received the divine nature of God in your spirit. You can do all things through Christ who strengthens you (Philippians 4:13)! If God told you to do something in His Word and did not give you the ability to do it, then He would not be God; He would be unjust. But God is just, and He wants you to win in life's battles.

So, what I'm about to share with you may be shocking. I believe it is from the Spirit of God, and it is scripturally backed up.

There are two things that you are going to have to maintain in order to fight the good fight of faith: (1) *the spirit of faith;* and (2) *a spirit of love and forgiveness.* In this chapter, I'm going to talk about the first key—maintaining the spirit of faith at all times. I'll talk about the second key in the next chapter.

## KEY NUMBER ONE: MAINTAIN THE SPIRIT OF FAITH

I say this with all humility, but very seldom do I find a preacher who has the spirit of faith as described in Second Corinthians 4:13.

Why do I make that kind of a statement? Because once a preacher—or *anybody*—opens his mouth and begins speaking, you can locate him. I know whether a person has the spirit of faith by the words that he speaks.

**We having the same spirit of faith, according as it is written, I believed, and therefore have I spoken; we also believe, and therefore speak.**

**2 CORINTHIANS 4:13**

Now, the potential for having the spirit of faith is in you if you are born again. But it has to be developed so it can operate in this earthly realm. A minister should make doubly sure that he takes ahold of the spirit of faith and develops it. He needs to have simplicity in his teaching, accuracy with the Scripture, a spirit of boldness and, of course, the anointing of God on his life. Then when he opens his mouth, it will be evident that he is operating in the spirit of faith.

You know, a minister can quote Scriptures all day long, but that doesn't mean he is operating in the spirit of faith. I remember when the wife of one of my board members first told me about a certain minister. I turned on my television so I could hear him. This minister came on and sang a song, "All the Way." I said, "That's me. I want to go all the way with God."

I saw that this minister was dressed right. The camera panned out into the crowd, and I saw that his church people looked prosperous. You could see the joy and victory on their faces. Then he began speaking, and I saw that he talked right. When I heard him speak, I said, "This brother has the spirit of faith." I told my wife, "Pack my bags, Honey. I need to go see this man. I want to talk with him." My wife said, "I believe that if the Lord wants you to meet him, you will get a chance to meet him." I wanted to go that day! But if I had gone, he probably would have said, "Leroy *who?*"

I watched him on TV three or four times before I finally had a chance to meet him, and he has turned out to be one of my best friends. We can sit down and talk for five hours, and we just *click.*

You see, when you are trying to speak revelation knowledge and you don't have the spirit of faith, boy, it is a harmful thing. You speak, and the people just say, "Yeah? So what." But when you speak to people with the spirit of faith, they will know it, and it is a good thing!

There are ministers with whom I have associated who were not operating in the spirit of faith. They were just as dull as they could be. I talked to them in a hurry and said, "I've got to go," because I didn't want that to rub off on me. But the Lord did lead me to hang around some of them, because I had the opportunity to rub off on *them.*

Religion, philosophy and the doctrines of men are the greatest enemies to the spirit of faith. People operating in religion, philosophy and the doctrines of men will say, "You can't do this. You can't do that." They have a defeatist attitude. Listening to somebody with that kind of mentality will keep you from entering the realm of the spirit of faith and winning over life's challenges.

Let me show you an Old Testament saint who operated in the spirit of faith. He had an excellent spirit operating in his life.

> **It pleased Darius to set over the kingdom an hundred and twenty princes, which should be over the whole kingdom; And over these three presidents; of whom Daniel was first: that the princes might give accounts unto them, and the king should have no damage. Then this Daniel was preferred above the presidents and princes, because an excellent spirit was in him; and the king thought to set him over the whole realm.**
>
> DANIEL 6:1-3

Note that Daniel was first—the top man—among the presidents and princes, who gave account unto him so that the king should have no damage or loss. Daniel was preferred above the presidents and princes! A strong statement in verse 3 tells us why: ...**because an excellent spirit was in him....**

You see, if you are going to fight the good fight of faith, you are not only going to have to have the spirit of faith, you are also going to have to have and maintain an excellent spirit. As I said, many believe they can't maintain an excellent spirit at all times, because they are so sin conscious. For example, somebody could be used of the Lord to sing an anointed song in church, and, afterward, people will tell him or her, "Wow! You really sang well this morning!" That person will try to *act* humble and say, "It wasn't me." Well, who was it, then? It *was* you—the person singing!

141

Certainly, God used that singer. That's what people are trying to say when they say, "It wasn't me." But God is not going to sing a song by Himself; He's going to use *people*.

## Glorify God and Refuse To Be Deceived by Religious Cliches

The best thing to do when someone compliments you about something is to say, "Well, praise the Lord. Glory to God." But, you see, people are so sin conscious, they are afraid to say, "Thank you. Glory be to God" when God uses them. They try to put it all off on God and act as if they themselves weren't even there!

These cliches we use trying to humble ourselves make us seem crazy! I mean, the Holy Spirit cannot sing by Himself! He needs an instrument, a voice. What I'm saying is that it's okay to have an excellent spirit, because you can't have an excellent spirit without the Lord. He is the reason you can have an excellent spirit! So just glorify Him with what He's given you and refuse to be deceived by religious cliches.

We have established that Daniel had an excellent spirit. Daniel, who was a slave in Babylon, became preferred and was put in a position above all of his colleagues because he had such a spirit of excellence in him. I want to ask you a question. Why shouldn't we—blood-bought, blood-washed saints of God with the same Spirit who raised Christ from the dead indwelling us—be able to have a spirit of excellence too? Why can't *we* cultivate and develop a spirit of excellence? We *can!* The Spirit that is in us is an excellent Spirit, but we will have to catch up with it by getting our souls right—by renewing our minds—and by taking control over our bodies.

Why can't people read a testimony somewhere when we leave this earth that we had an excellent spirit? There is no reason why we can't have an excellent spirit today. We should be known through the annals of time as Saint Leroy, Saint Charles, Saint Joe and so forth. But instead of taking our places as *saints,* many of us are just content to be *ain'ts!*

When we are born again, we are all saints. We thought that "saint" meant *sinless.* But in the new birth, "saint" means our sins have been paid for. So when they call us saints, it doesn't mean that we are free from sin in ourselves (although we should not be practicing sin). It just means that we are sinless because of Jesus. He paid the price, and we are re-created in Him. We have been given the ability to have a spirit of excellence.

## AN EXCELLENT SPIRIT DEFINED

Daniel was preferred above the presidents and princes because an excellent spirit was in him. Now, what is an excellent spirit? It is living up to your highest potential. You know, very few of us are really doing that. As Christians, we have God's Spirit in us, and His Spirit is certainly excellent. Therefore, the spirit of excellence is in us. That spirit will help us live to our highest potential here in the earth's realm, "preferred" and "above" presidents and princes!

Just think what would happen if each one of us would decide to operate in the spirit of excellence. Well, if you are going to operate in the spirit of excellence, you are also going to have to operate in the spirit of faith and in a spirit of love and forgiveness.

Notice Daniel 6:3 again:

> **Then this Daniel was preferred above the presidents and princes, because an excellent spirit was in him; and the king thought to set him over the whole realm.**
>
> DANIEL 6:3

Now, why do we often see one Christian excelling above another one? You might say, "God is not fair." But, often, the case is, you are not fair to *yourself,* because you are not living up to your highest potential. If you are always defeated and whipped, never having any victory, it is not God's fault. God has already established the faith fight for you—the means whereby you can overcome challenges and defeat. He told you that you must please Him by faith, receive from Him by faith and walk by faith as a lifestyle. In other words, you must sleep in faith, eat in faith, talk in faith and do everything in faith. The Bible says that the just shall *live* by faith.

Now, if you want to be stupid and forget about faith, just go ahead and be stupid and let the devil ride "shotgun" with you in life. But you really need to rise up in faith and tell him to get off your wagon! Just stop the wagon, so to speak, and say, "Mr. Devil, this is your stop. Get off this wagon. You are just extra baggage, and I don't have to put up with this mess."

You have the ability to fight the good fight of faith, but it's something that *you* will have to do. No one else can do it for you.

## GOD WILL PUT YOU OVER!

Now, notice in Daniel 6 that the king put Daniel over the whole realm. I want you to look at that in relation to your own life. If you will develop and maintain an excellent spirit, God will put you over! God will put you above! God will put you in a position of being preferred! God will put you first! And no matter how many of us are operating in a spirit of excellence, when God is in it, we can *all* be first!

When you talk to entrepreneurs and those who are "making it" in life, they will tell you that there is a lot of room at the top. It is crowded at the bottom and in between, yet so many Christians are just trying to get themselves a little space in the scheme of things. They are all in the middle seat, where it's tight and crowded. If they would determine that they're going to go all the way with God, they could go to the top, where they could have plenty of room to swing their arms and be happy!

So many pastors refuse to cultivate the spirit of excellence. They won't rise up and do things in the way God wants them carried out. So God is not going to put His children in their churches. Most of the people who are in their churches are just sticking to family tradition and heritage. They are staying there and "sinking with the ship." Some of them even want to leave, but they won't, because those family ties are so strong. They say, "I just have to stay with this church." They never cultivate the spirit of excellence.

Many do not even know that they can have a spirit of excellence. They may have read the whole Bible and missed that verse in Daniel. Many in the Church will not permit the word "excellent" to touch them! They have the mistaken idea that we are all just trying to make it, some way, somehow.

But that is not what the Bible teaches. The Bible teaches us to fight the good fight of faith with an excellent spirit and to win in life's challenges.

## From Pressure to Promotion

I want to show you how to realize the fulfillment of the dreams God has given you even when pressure comes and it doesn't look as if you are going to fulfill those dreams. Remember in Genesis 37 God had given Joseph a dream; but before Joseph realized his dream, he went to the pit, where his jealous brothers threw him, leaving him for dead.

Then Joseph was sold into slavery and went to the palace, where he was made keeper of the house by Potiphar. He was then falsely accused by the man's wife, who was not a nice girl, and he was thrown into prison. Of course, Joseph had an excellent spirit in him, and he was finally promoted to be second in command only to Pharaoh. (See Genesis 41:40-43.) So in the midst of great *pressure,* Joseph went from the *pit* to the *palace* to the *prison* to *Pharaoh!* He was knocked down repeatedly, but he couldn't stay down! He had an excellent spirit in him, and in the midst of *pressure,* God *promoted* him!

There is a valuable lesson to learn here in the story of Joseph. You see, if you do not act right in the pit, you will never get to the palace. Then if you do not know how to handle pressure in the palace, and even in prison, you will never get to "Pharaoh," or to the throne. You will never be promoted by God the way He wants to promote you.

—∞— HOW TO DEAL WITH PRESSURE —∞—

At some time or another, pressure comes against all of us. We need to learn how to deal with pressure. We need to be able to punch a hole in the "balloon" of pressure and let all the air—all the pressure—come out!

Well, how easy is it to burst a balloon? I mean, if you just stick a pin in it, it pops. Once you learn to operate in a spirit of excellence, dealing with your pressures will become just like bursting a balloon. And the "pin" that you use for life's pressures is the Word of God. In fact, God did not give you a *pin*—He gave you a *sword!* Can you burst a balloon with a sword? I mean, all you have to do is just drop the sword on the balloon, and that balloon will burst wide open! That is the way we are to deal with the pressures of life—with the sword of the Spirit, which is the Word of God (Ephesians 6:17). Also, I'm sure you've noticed what a loud noise a popping balloon makes. Well, the pressures of life sometimes make a lot of noise too. But when the noise of the pressure is the loudest, that means it is on its way out!

When you are dealing with pressure—when a situation gets tighter and tighter—that is not the time to quit. The devil is just putting on the squeeze. You see, you are about to get him and his pressure off of

146

you, and he is going to make a lot of noise as you do. But you just keep at it with the Word of God. You take that sword and say, "Pow!" Don't ever say, "The devil's got me." No, you say, "I've got *him*."

You see, when you pop a balloon of pressure in your life and a loud noise goes off, the pressure is off. But the devil tries to get people to believe that the noise means the pressure is bigger than ever—that the situation is worse and that they've got more problems. Yet, the noise was really the thing that opened the door and set those people free. But because of wrong thinking, they will stick around, believing the devil's lies while he blows up another balloon for them to deal with!

Jesus ministered in simplicity. If you read the Gospels, you'll notice that Jesus used simple things to teach the people. He could not use complicated things to teach them, because they constantly would have had to be figuring stuff out.

When the devil is on you, you do not have time to figure anything out. But you can think about a balloon. You can say, "Oh! I know what this is. I read about it in Reverend Thompson's book. It's a balloon. I believe I'll just burst this thing!" You can say to your friend who's facing pressure, "Girl, I read a book and found out that this is nothing but a balloon we are dealing with. Let's handle it."

Your friend might come from a traditional church, and she might say, "You're crazy. We can't do anything about this!" But God can, and He said that His Word would accomplish whatever it is sent out to do (Isaiah 55:11), including the bursting of "balloons"! And in the case of pressures in our bodies, sickness and disease try to come to us in big balloons with all kinds of names on them. But we can burst them with the Word of God too!

What are you dealing with today? Whatever is binding you is a balloon with devilish air in it. So take out your sword and burst that problem.

You know, there are many kinds of pressures that come to us in life. For example, Joseph first encountered pressure from his brothers, who were jealous of him. Then he had the pressure of that woman, Potiphar's wife. Every day she said, "I'm going to get you; you're mine. You are going to sleep with me. You can bank on it—I'm yours, and you're mine."

## THE PRESSURE OF TEMPTATION

These kinds of pressures are relevant to us today, including those who are in the ministry. Some people lose whole ministries, and some people lose good spouses, because of the pressure of temptation. *Pressure!* You can't go to the top if you can't stand pressure. You have to learn how to run! I've run before. For instance, I came out of a restaurant once, and a woman followed me out, saying, "You're a fine specimen of a man." I said, "Thank you," and just kept walking toward my car. I had a new Cadillac at the time. That woman said, "And, oh, that is a fine car. I could see myself riding in that car."

I tried to be polite and humble. I said, "Ma'am, I am a preacher of the Gospel." She just said, "Oh," and got closer to me. I thought that when I told her I was a preacher, she would back off. But she didn't; she came on to me even more. So I jumped into my car and got out of there!

In the ministry and in life, you have to know how to deal with pressure, including the pressure of temptation. Now, if you were a dead man, and a good-looking woman got in your face, you wouldn't have any problems. But since you are alive, you'd better know how to run and get yourself away from that temptation.

## NEEDLESS TEMPTATIONS

While I'm on the subject of temptation, I need to talk to you about needless temptation. Sometimes people miss it over a temptation that shouldn't even have been there to start with. For example, sometimes when a husband messes up, it is partially the wife's responsibility. (Some women don't want to hear that, because they don't want to take any of the responsibility.) For example, I know a pastor who went astray, whose wife was never at home. She was busy running all over the world, leaving her husband behind with women tapping him on the shoulder every day. If this man's wife had been home, those taps would not have meant anything. Those taps might not have become temptations.

So, you wives, it doesn't matter whether you feel like it or not, take care of your husbands. And it goes both ways. You husbands, learn not to think just about yourselves. Both husbands and wives need to take responsibility for the stability and well-being of their families and homes.

## THE COMMITMENT TO EXCELLENCE

It takes an excellent spirit to withstand the pressure of temptation. It takes someone committed to God wholeheartedly to run when temptation presents itself. Daniel was that kind of person.

> **But Daniel purposed in his heart that he would not defile himself with the portion of the king's meat, nor with the wine which he drank: therefore he requested of the prince of the eunuchs that he might not defile himself.**
>
> DANIEL 1:8

In this verse, we can see something that a person with an excellent spirit carries: commitment and determination to do God's will and not to be distracted by temptation and the trappings of the world. That kind of commitment comes from the heart. The spirit of faith and a spirit of love and forgiveness are attitudes of the heart, not of the head. Notice, it says, **Daniel purposed in his HEART that he** would not defile himself with the portion of the king's meat, nor with the wine which he drank.... Daniel purposed in his *heart*, not in his *head*, that he would not defile himself or give in to the pressure of temptation.

You see, faith is of the heart. When you fight the good fight of faith, you fight with the Word of God in your heart and in your mouth—with your confession. Maintaining an excellent spirit is a heart issue. If you will guard your heart, keep it from unforgiveness and keep it tender before God, it will not *weaken* you, as people in the world believe. No, it will *strengthen* you and enable you to overcome in life's fights.

# Chapter 9

## *How To Maintain an Excellent Spirit in the Midst of Temptation, Part 2*

One of the greatest hindrances to faith—one of the things that will shut your faith down the quickest and cause the most faith failures—is unforgiveness. You could be in the middle of a good faith fight, just about to win it; but if you let unforgiveness creep in, it will shut your faith fight down, and the enemy will whip you in that circumstance.

In order to fight the faith fight successfully, you not only have to know how to stand your ground, remaining in faith despite all opposition, but you also have to know how to maintain an excellent spirit in the midst of your challenge. That includes knowing how to maintain a spirit of love and forgiveness.

### KEY NUMBER TWO:
### MAINTAIN A SPIRIT OF LOVE AND FORGIVENESS

In the last chapter, I talked about two keys to winning over a faith challenge. The first key *is maintaining the spirit of faith at all times.* The second key is *maintaining a spirit of love and forgiveness at all costs.*

Maintaining a spirit of love and forgiveness at all costs means that it doesn't matter what you have to "take" to stay in a good spirit, you will do it. You will keep a good spirit no matter how many kicks, licks, evil words or rolling eyes that you get!

You see, it takes *effort* to maintain the spirit of forgiveness. But being able to forgive when someone has wronged you is spiritual. In other words, you will never be able to handle it in your flesh. The flesh says, "Hit back" or "Curse back." The flesh says, "Dig a pit for them just like they dug for you." So we cannot forgive in the flesh as God forgives. We forgive in our spirits, or hearts, with the help of the Holy Spirit. As Christians, we have the capability to forgive.

Many times, I have referred to what Jesus said, "If someone smacks you on one cheek, you turn the other cheek" (Matthew 5:39; Luke 6:29), by saying, "I'm not too excited about turning the other cheek in situations where someone hits me." But, actually, Jesus wasn't necessarily talking about someone literally hitting you. He was talking about maintaining a spirit of forgiveness. Most "licks" are harder when no one even touches you. I mean, it can hurt worse when someone puts a "licking" on you with their words.

## ⸻ YOU CAN FORGIVE! ⸻

Have you ever been in a position where you had to forgive somebody? (You have, or you're lying about it. Or maybe you've been living on Mars or somewhere else where there aren't any people!) You *can* forgive whether you feel as if you can or not.

**And Jesus answering saith unto them, Have faith in God. For verily I say unto you, That whosoever shall say unto this mountain, Be thou removed, and be thou cast into**

the sea; and shall not doubt in his heart, but shall believe that those things which he saith shall come to pass; he shall have whatsoever he saith. Therefore I say unto you, What things soever ye desire, when ye pray, believe that ye receive them, and ye shall have them. And when ye stand praying, forgive, if ye have ought against any: that your Father also which is in heaven may forgive you your trespasses. But if ye do not forgive, neither will your Father which is in heaven forgive your trespasses.

MARK 11:22-26

In this passage, Jesus explains the divine ability that He has placed in us to believe things in our hearts, say them with our mouths and have them come to pass. Believing with the heart and speaking with the mouth causes "creation." Jesus explained this divine system, or pattern, by dealing with a fig tree (vv. 12,14). He was showing us that we have the ability to create our own world, our own circumstances, in spite of what is going on around us in the natural. But within the context of this system is a very important factor that you must implement in order for this divine pattern to work. That ingredient is the spirit of forgiveness.

Mark 11:22-24 deals with faith and how to use it. But Mark 11:25 and 26 hold a greater significance to using your faith effectively than most people realize.

Mark 11:22 establishes the fact that you have God's kind of faith. You have the faith of God in you. A statement in Romans 12:3 backs up that fact:

...God hath dealt to every man the measure of faith.

So we know that we have God's kind of faith. What does God's kind of faith consist of? It consists of believing in your heart and confessing with your mouth, calling things that be not as though

153

they were and creating what you desire. But it also consists of walking in love and forgiveness.

**AND when ye stand praying, forgive, if ye have ought against any: that your Father also which is in heaven may forgive you your trespasses.**

MARK 11:25

As I said, one of the greatest hindrances to having God's kind of faith is unforgiveness. And what the enemy does when you are in a good faith fight is to come at you using somebody to rub you the wrong way, whether it be at home or on the job, through a boss or co-worker or a spouse, parent, child, niece, nephew, aunt, uncle, grandparent or godparent! How you handle the situation will determine whether you remain in the fight.

You might be busy thinking you've got a faith fight going on, and you won't pay any attention to the fact that the devil is going to present you with an opportunity to get into unforgiveness. If you miss it, you could handle the situation wrong, and your faith will get shut down. That's why it's so important to establish in your heart that you are going to have a spirit of forgiveness no matter what anybody else does to you.

You know, when someone wrongs you, for a while, it "ruffles" you. But your spirit man will come and say, "Look, what is this to you?" and will lead you back into a place spiritually where you can walk with God and maintain a strong spirit of faith. When you are following your heart and not your flesh, you won't become all upset and be fighting like the person who is coming against you. In the faith walk, you cannot afford to make enemies by refusing to walk in love and forgiveness.

I tell you, life itself can be a challenge, a contest, at times. But Jesus tells us how to handle challenges. He said, **Have faith in God.**

In the Greek, that means, "Have the faith of God" or "Have God's kind of faith."

Then Jesus goes on to say in Mark 11:23, **For verily I say unto you, That whosoever shall say unto this mountain, Be thou removed, and be thou cast into the sea; and shall not doubt in his heart, but shall believe that those things which he saith shall come to pass; he shall have whatsoever he saith.**

In Romans 4, Abraham decided he was going to take this same pattern from God, because, after all, he was made in God's own image. God called those things that were not as though they were.

> **Therefore it is of faith, that it might be by grace; to the end the promise might be sure to all the seed; not to that only which is of the law, but to that also which is of the faith of Abraham; who is the father of us all, (As it is written, I have made thee a father of many nations,) before him whom he believed, even God, who quickeneth the dead, and calleth those things which be not as though they were.**
>
> ROMANS 4:16,17

Abraham began to pattern himself after God by calling those things that were not as though they were.

> **Who against hope believed in hope, that he might become the father of many nations, according to that which was spoken, So shall thy seed be. And being not weak in faith, he considered not his own body now dead, when he was about an hundred years old, neither yet the deadness of Sara's womb: He staggered not at the promise of God through unbelief; but was strong in faith, giving glory to God; And being fully persuaded, that what he had promised, he was able also to perform.**
>
> ROMANS 4:18-21

155

You see, we have the capability of walking by faith and not by sight—believing with our hearts and confessing with our mouths what we believe. And our faith confessions create realities; they create the finished products in our lives.

### DON'T ALLOW YOUR FAITH TO BE SHUT DOWN

So we know we have the ability to call those things that be not as though they were, according to Mark 11 and Romans 4. However, many times we are doing a lot of calling, but nothing is coming forth. That's because somewhere in the system of faith, we have shut our faith down.

### UNFORGIVENESS GRIEVES THE HOLY SPIRIT

Listen, when you are in unforgiveness, you grieve the Holy Spirit. He is your helper, your standby. I believe one reason a dove is a symbol of the Holy Spirit is to let us know that as soon as we get into a spirit of unforgiveness, it grieves Him, and He will fly away, so to speak.

You cannot make a lot of noise or quick movements around a bird, or it will fly away. It's the same way with the Holy Spirit when you walk in unforgiveness. Now, that does not mean that the Holy Spirit leaves you. Jesus said that He would abide with us forever (John 14:16). But as soon as you grieve the Holy Spirit, you become naked spiritually. It's like having no clothes on in the middle of the town square! But when the Holy Spirit has been grieved, He is not talking. He is not helping. He is not singing. Therefore, you have no song. You are just "dry, dead and cold." (Every one of us has been there at one time or another.)

We know that Mark 11:25 and 26 tell us that unforgiveness makes verses 22 through 24 null and void—inoperative. Unforgiveness will quickly grieve the Holy Spirit. So we need to study these verses and know something about them.

Too many people have been believing and confessing things, but haven't been receiving anything. They know the formula: Believe with the heart; confess with the mouth. But the Bible says in James 3:11 that good water and bad water can't come out of the same fountain (or the same *faucet,* in modern language). In other words, if you are believing and confessing something from God's Word on the one hand, but on the other hand, you are talking against others and letting corrupt communication proceed out of your mouth (Ephesians 4:29); you are either slowing your faith down or shutting your faith down, depending on how far you've gone with disobeying God in that area.

When you shut your faith down, sometimes you have to start all over again. But if you've missed it, you need to repent and get back on your faith, maintaining a spirit of love and forgiveness.

Since the Bible says to let no corrupt communication proceed out of your mouth, that means you have a choice. You are going to be presented with the temptation to talk corrupt talk, but you can stop those things from coming out of your mouth.

## YOUR FLESH WILL TELL YOU NOT TO FORGIVE

Actually, the more you get into the things of God, the more chances you are going to have to get into unforgiveness. When the temptation not to forgive is presented to some people, they would rather, in their *flesh,* go with the unforgiveness. They will go through all kinds of foolishness, because they don't understand what the Bible says about the sufferings of Christ.

**That I [Paul] may know him [Jesus], and the power of his resurrection, and the fellowship of his sufferings, being made conformable unto his death.**

PHILIPPIANS 3:10

Maintaining an excellent spirit can be hard on the flesh. For example, if someone has wronged you, your flesh doesn't want to forgive him or her. As I said in the last chapter, forgiveness and walking in God's kind of love (and God's kind of faith) are of the heart, or spirit; they are not of the flesh.

I heard Brother Hagin give an illustration along this line. He was talking about the time he had just started pastoring a certain church years ago, and a woman in the congregation went to his parsonage to introduce herself and to tell him all about another woman in the church who had mistreated her. Brother Hagin thought the incident had just happened the previous week, so he asked her about it, and she said it had happened years ago. Brother Hagin said he almost "fell out," because he thought she was talking about something that had happened recently. That woman had let that unforgiveness boil in her for all those years! She was walking in the flesh, not in the Spirit.

## THE GREATER ONE WILL HELP YOU FORGIVE

I know there are people who have been horribly mistreated by others, even by loved ones. I am in no way making light of that fact. Maybe you were misused as a child by a relative. Maybe your husband beat you and left you and the kids to make it on your own. But whatever happened to you, you need to forgive those who wronged you. You *can* do it. The Bible says you can. And you can do it today; you don't have to wait. You can simply decide to do it, and the greater One who lives inside of you will help you.

Then when you forgive, you can get back in the faith fight and move those mountains and obstacles that have been standing in your way. You can get some things changed that need to be changed. With a spirit of love and forgiveness, nobody can ride piggyback on your spirit. In other words, no one, including the devil, can bind you up anymore and stop you from receiving what you need or want from God. You can operate in complete freedom.

## DON'T BEGRUDGE THE MINISTER WHO TELLS THE TRUTH!

Sometimes people even get in unforgiveness against their pastors or other ministers, especially if they say something to them that they do not want to hear. They don't want to receive it, so they get mad at the preacher. But most of the time he's just trying to give them the truth; he just wants to help them. But they're in unforgiveness, and their faith is shut down. It's inoperative.

If you get mad at the man of God and begin grumbling and carrying on, God is not going to bless you. If you're mad at the preacher for telling you the truth, you need to straighten up! He's just the "mailman," anyway. He is just delivering what God has told him to deliver! And he's human. Sometimes he may put the "mail" in the wrong "box." He can miss it just like you can. So walk in a spirit of forgiveness toward others, even ministers.

You may have been carrying around unforgiveness for years. Today is your day. Simply give that to the Lord. Every time the enemy tries to bring it up and remind you of how so-and-so hurt you, you tell him that you are not going to let him exalt anything against the knowledge of God. Second Corinthians 10:5 says, **Casting down imaginations, and every high thing that exalteth itself against the**

159

knowledge of God, and bringing into captivity every thought to the obedience of Christ.

## RACE ISSUES CAN BE AN UNFORGIVENESS TRAP

You know, sometimes there is a racial issue that hinders people and causes them to stumble in their faith fight. Sometimes white folks are in unforgiveness toward black folks, and black folks are in unforgiveness toward white folks. A black man might say, "Yes, but the white man has wronged us."

If you are black, white folks do not owe you anything. And you do not owe them anything. That is the past. All of it was devilish, and none of us were there. You were not there, and I was not there. (If you were there, you must be kin to Methuselah!)

So let's get rid of all these old unforgiveness issues. Sure, your flesh will try to bring something up, because that is the devil working against you. He will try to oppress you and get you to turn to the flesh. Tell him to stop! Tell him, "I am born again. I have a new spirit, a spirit of love and forgiveness."

I tell you, I pastor an integrated church which includes black and white folks. And there are both black and white men in my church whom I would trust "with my back." In other words, they will cover me, even with my back turned, and I know I can trust them. I know they love me. I know they are faithful to me as their pastor. I know that if anybody tried to get to me, he would have to go through them first before he could get to me.

You just can't afford to let anything stop the mighty streaming flow of the Spirit of God in your life and the love of God in your heart. You can't afford to let anything trip you up in your faith fight.

I love *people*—no matter what their races or colors! And I believe that allowing the love of God to motivate me in all that I do is the reason my ministry is so successful today.

Let's continue reading in Philippians 3:10:

**That I may know him, and the power of his resurrection, and the fellowship of his sufferings, being made conformable unto his death.**

Paul said, "That I may know Him and the power of His resurrection." But Paul didn't know when to quit! He should have stopped right there and gone on to verse 11. But he messed the whole thing up! He added to the sentence, **...and the fellowship of His sufferings....**

## FOLLOWING JESUS' EXAMPLE— THE PRICE OF KNOWING HIM

Someone said, "Well, I like the part about Jesus' power and His resurrection." But in order to know Him and the power of His resurrection, you're going to have to deal with the fellowship of His sufferings. What is the fellowship of His sufferings? That's talking about being able to stand the test when persecution and other things come against you as a believer.

You see, Jesus said you are going to be persecuted because you are a Christian (Matthew 5:10,11). Jesus went through a lot of things. People came against Him, but He stood the test. And He wants us to stand the test in the same way—in a forgiving spirit.

Let me show you Jesus in vivid color in Luke 23. Let's see how He handled the most crucial moment of His life on earth.

**Pilate therefore, willing to release Jesus, spake again to them. But they cried, saying, Crucify him, crucify him. And he [Pilate] said unto them the third time, Why, what evil**

hath he done? I have found no cause of death in him: I will therefore chastise him, and let him go. And they were instant with loud voices, requiring that he might be crucified. And the voices of them and of the chief priests prevailed.

LUKE 23:20-23

That same group that had once hollered, "Hosanna! Hosanna!" were now hollering, "Crucify Him! Crucify Him!" Not many days before, they had spread palm branches across Jesus' path so He could walk on them. Some took off their outer garments for the Master. But not long after that, they were yelling, "Crucify Him!" Now, you know the words "crucify Him" don't sound anything like "Hosanna"!

## "FORGIVE THEM, FOR THEY KNOW NOT WHAT THEY DO"

The people whom Jesus was sent to save came against Him, but He gave us a revelation of how to handle those kinds of situations. On the cross of Calvary, when even His disciples had turned their backs on Him, Jesus stood the test and kept His spirit calm and cool. With spikes nailed into His hands and feet, and His side pierced, He had a spirit of forgiveness. It was the worst possible condition. I mean, if He were like some of us, Jesus would have been cursing, saying, "Somebody, get me a gun! I want to shoot every guard here!" Jesus was human, too, but He remained sinless as He walked on the earth. He overrode those thoughts that undoubtedly came to Him to try to get Him to fight back.

Let's look at verses 33 and 34:

And when they were come to the place, which is called Calvary, there they crucified him, and the malefactors, one on the right hand, and the other on the left. Then said

162

**Jesus, Father, FORGIVE THEM; for they know not what they do. And they parted his raiment, and cast lots.**

When Jesus said, "Father, forgive them," He was setting an example for us to follow. When others mistreat us and come against us, we should have the same attitude. We should say, "Father, forgive them, for they know not what they do." Actually, when someone messes with a child of God, a member of the Body of Christ, he is really messing with the Lord. I can prove that by the Bible. Look at Acts 9.

> **And as he [Saul] journeyed, he came near Damascus: and suddenly there shined round about him a light from heaven: And he fell to the earth, and heard a voice saying unto him, Saul, Saul, why persecutest thou me? And he said, Who art thou, Lord? And the Lord said, I am Jesus whom thou persecutest: it is hard for thee to kick against the pricks.**
>
> ACTS 9:3-5

This passage is talking about Saul's conversion. He had been persecuting Christians as a devout religious Hebrew. In verse 4, after Saul had been blinded and had fallen to the ground, the Lord said unto him, **Saul, Saul, why persecutest thou ME?** Then Paul said, **Who art thou, Lord? And the Lord said, I am Jesus WHOM THOU PERSECUTEST: it is hard for thee to kick against the pricks.**

You see, Paul had been coming against the Church, against Christians, but the Lord took it personally. The Lord didn't ask Saul, "Why art thou persecuting so-and-so in the Church?" No, He said, "Why are you persecuting *Me?*"

So, you see, when someone comes against a child of God, he is coming against the Lord. If he really knew that it was the Lord he was coming against, he probably would not be doing it. In effect, Jesus said on the cross, "Father, forgive them, for I know that if they really knew what they were doing, they would not be doing this! They don't know who I am. They don't know how tight You and I are, Father. They don't know what they're doing."

I have practiced that attitude myself over the years. When somebody tries to mess with me, I cry out to the Lord, saying, "Oh, Lord, they don't know what they are doing. Forgive them, Lord. Help them to see. Lord, tell them to stop! This is my prayer for them. Stop them, because they are getting themselves into trouble."

When you mess with a King's kid who's walking uprightly, God tells Jesus, "Hey, he's messing with Us now!" I tell you, you don't want to mess with the Lord! If you read the Old Testament, you'll find that He wiped out whole tribes. I mean, He just let the earth open up, and all the foundation of their houses started going under! They hollered, "Help!" But it was too late then. They'd already gotten the Man disturbed!

You see, I pray for a person before he gets the Man disturbed. Getting you or me disturbed is all right, but getting the Man, Jesus Christ, disturbed is another story altogether. People sometimes die early messing with God's kids, coming against them and hurting them.

So we know from the Bible that Christians will face persecution and opposition in life. But Jesus also told us how to handle it. He said, "Forgive them, for they know not what they do."

### UNFORGIVENESS WILL STOP THE FLOW OF GOD'S POWER IN YOUR LIFE

Something else I want you to see is this: In the midst of Jesus' situation on that cross, He said, "Forgive them." But if Jesus hadn't forgiven them, He would have stopped the resurrection! If He couldn't have forgiven His enemies—those who opposed and crucified Him—the resurrection couldn't have gone forward. None of us as believers today would be where we are today. There would be no Kingdom of God for us to enter.

Do you see how important it is to release your enemies—those who come against and persecute you? We have to forgive so the work of God can go on—so it can go forward in our lives!

Jesus could not have fought the good fight of faith and stood His ground in doing all of God's will with unforgiveness in His heart against those who crucified Him. In other words, if Jesus had not had the spirit of forgiveness and maintained an excellent spirit, even right there on the cross, the resurrection would not have taken place! Why? Because *unforgiveness stops the power of God from working on your behalf!* You know that if Jesus had to walk in love and forgiveness to keep the power of God working on His behalf, we are going to have to walk in love too!

It doesn't matter how many good confessions you are making, what church you attend or how many specials you sing in the choir, if you have unforgiveness in your heart, you are not doing anything for the Kingdom of God! You are just making noise like those tinkling cymbals First Corinthians 13:1 talks about.

## RECOGNIZING AND RESISTING UNFORGIVENESS BETWEEN SPOUSES

I know the enemy is especially interested in causing problems between husbands and wives. Sometimes they will even come to church squabbling. Then when they get in the service, they don't have ears to hear, eyes to see or hearts to understand what the Spirit of God is saying, and they leave church in the same condition *or worse* than they were in when they left home.

Years ago, I learned a secret to keep from having those kinds of squabbles on the way to church. I wouldn't *talk!* As First Corinthians

14:1 says in *The Amplified Bible,* I purposed to make love my very quest. I'm a little more mature now, so I talk a little more. But I remember, at one time, I wouldn't say anything! (I actually know of pastors who would lock themselves in their dens or studies almost all day on Saturdays while they were studying so they wouldn't get in those squabbles and hinder their ability to hear from God!)

We have to realize that we wrestle not with flesh and blood, but with principalities, powers, rulers of the darkness of this world and spiritual wickedness in high places (Ephesians 6:12). The enemy tries to start arguments. But we don't have to yield to him or listen to him. We can walk in love and forgiveness.

You may have been trying to walk in love and forgiveness in your own strength, because you want to live right. But it's the *Holy Spirit* who gives you the ability to forgive when there's no forgiveness in sight and there's seemingly no way around a situation. So in order to live in the spirit of forgiveness, you have to have the Holy Spirit helping you.

## DO WHAT'S RIGHT AND STAY IN THE FLOW OF THE SPIRIT

Even though you may want to do what's right, sometimes people just rub you the wrong way or provoke you in some way. Well, if that happens to you and you wrong someone as a result, you're going to have to go back to that person and make it right. Actually, it's better not to do wrong to begin with, but if you *do* mess up, it's better to get it straight right away. Don't wait to make something straight. It hurts more when you have to go back than it does when you get it straight at the very first! The first hurt isn't as bad as the second hurt—as having to go back and bow, so to speak.

When you mistreat a person, you have to go back to him or her if you want an excellent spirit and if you want to walk in the blessings of God. I've had to go back and say to people, "Man, I'm wrong. Forgive me." And that's not easy on the flesh. Some pastors think they don't ever need to apologize to anyone. But they do need to—if they want to stay in the flow of the Holy Spirit.

It's the Holy Spirit who gives you the ability to forgive and to stay in the faith fight! You will have plenty of opportunities to get in unforgiveness and to lose your faith fights, but if you determine to do what's right and rely on the Holy Spirit, you will win over all the challenges of life.

I learned an important truth along this line years ago from a respected minister. It's found in John 20.

> **Then said Jesus to them again, Peace be unto you: as my Father hath sent me, even so send I you. And when he had said this, he breathed on them, and saith unto them, Receive ye the Holy Ghost.**
>
> JOHN 20:21,22

Look at verse 21. Jesus said, **Peace be unto you: as my Father hath sent me, even so send I you.** Well, how did the Father send Jesus? The Father sent Jesus in the spirit of forgiveness. He had a forgiving spirit; He had a loving spirit. He went through some *mess* with those religious folks, the Pharisees and Sadducees. I mean, they gave Jesus trouble! But Jesus walked in a forgiving spirit.

—∞— "Be Angry and Sin Not" —∞—

Now, keep in mind that the Bible did not say you can't be angry. Paul wrote that it is possible to "be angry and sin not" (Ephesians 4:26). There is a holy indignation that can rise up in you sometimes, but that doesn't mean you have to sin. You're not to let that anger become a part of you.

Sometimes you have to deal with things when there's holy indignation. But you can do it in the Spirit, with an excellent spirit. You don't have to do it in the flesh.

When people see a Christian deal with things this way, and he has to get a little rough, they will say, "I thought he was saved!" But he *is* saved. Just because someone becomes angry does not mean he is sinning. Do you remember Jesus in the temple with that whip (Matthew 21:12; Mark 11:15; Luke 19:45)? Jesus was "saved," wasn't He? He was the sinless Son of God, yet He drove those money changers out of the house of God.

I'm not saying that in our situations and circumstances we have to deal with things in that same way as a first resort. But sometimes we do have to get some things straight. If an unsaved person came into one of my church services and wanted to take over the service, my ushers would try to talk with him and pray with him to get him saved. Then if the person were still unruly, the ushers are trained to handle it, and they would handle it. They would escort that person out of the service and continue to try to pray with him. But if he wouldn't listen, they would instruct him to leave the premises. Now, if my ushers ever have to tell a person to leave, that wouldn't mean they weren't walking in love. It would just mean they were handling things so that there could be order in the church.

Someone might say, "Well, that doesn't sound too good. I mean, after all, we are Christians." But don't you understand that folks who are not saved cannot understand Christian ethics? You've got to handle them firmly sometimes. That's why I tell my congregation, "If you ever see anyone being escorted out of a service, just keep on listening to the minister, and pray quietly in tongues. Don't fret about it. The only reason they are being taken out of the service is that they won't listen to instruction and reason."

There is a way to be effective and to operate your life decently and in order with an excellent spirit. We don't have to go the world's way. We walk by faith, in the Spirit. And when the world says, "Fight back," we maintain a spirit of love and forgiveness.

## UNFORGIVENESS IS UNPRODUCTIVE

Have you ever been in unforgiveness? What did it do for you? Unforgiveness will do something for you, all right, but it doesn't do anything good! It makes you sick. It makes you confused. And it can make you broke! If you are a businessman, for example, and you're in unforgiveness, you won't have the wisdom of God as you did before. You will do crazy things in your business that you wouldn't ordinarily do, because you are confused. Just remember this: Unforgiveness always works *against* you. It never works *for* you.

What works for you in life, especially in the midst of challenges and temptations, is walking in love and forgiveness and maintaining an excellent spirit.

**Whose soever sins ye REMIT, they are remitted unto them; and whose soever sins ye RETAIN, they are retained.**

JOHN 20:23

I want you to pay attention to those two words "remit" and "retain." This verse is saying a lot of things, but one beautiful thing it reveals is that, because you as a believer have the Holy Spirit and the divine nature of God in you, you have the ability to release, or forgive, someone when he sins against you. Or you could do it the wrong way and retain that person's sin—you could walk in unforgiveness. If you do that, you'll have sin in *you* too!

In other words, I have the ability to *release* the sin or to *keep* the sin that someone commits against me. John 20:23 is also talking about hearing the Gospel, seeing the truth and coming out from under sin. But by the same token, I see in this verse that if a person mistreats me, I need to forgive him, and I have the *ability* to forgive him. But if I *don't* forgive him, *both* of us are in trouble! The person who mistreated me *committed* the sin—and I *kept* the sin! The seed of sin is in me as well as in him. But, if I go ahead and release that person, he is released. What he does after that is between him and God. That person could continue to sin if he chooses to, but because I forgive, I am free!

Let's look again at our golden text, Mark 11:22-25, and see further how a successful *faith* life is closely related to a successful love walk.

> **And Jesus answering saith unto them, Have faith in God. For verily I say unto you, That whosoever shall say unto this mountain, Be thou removed, and be thou cast into the sea; and shall not doubt in his heart, but shall believe that those things which he saith shall come to pass; he shall have whatsoever he saith. Therefore I say unto you, What things soever ye desire, when ye pray, believe that ye receive them, and ye shall have them. And when ye stand praying, forgive, if ye have ought against any: that your Father also which is in heaven may forgive you your trespasses.**
>
> MARK 11:22-25

There are three "phases" to this passage in Mark 11. *First,* Jesus is telling us to have the faith of God, or God's kind of faith (v. 22). *Second,* He is telling us how to talk and pray and use God's kind of faith (vv. 23,24). And, *third,* He is telling us how not to mess up (v. 25)!

> **And when ye stand praying, FORGIVE, if ye have ought against any: that your Father also which is in heaven may forgive you your trespasses.**
>
> MARK 11:25

170

Notice the word "forgive" in this verse. Jesus was telling us how not to mess up once we have begun standing our ground in faith. Jesus said, in effect, "When you stand praying and using your faith, *forgive.*" He said to forgive if you have *anything* against *anyone!*

Then Jesus said, "Forgive, that your Father in heaven may also forgive *your* trespasses." In other words, if you want to be forgiven, you need to forgive. God shows us in verse 26 the consequences of unforgiveness:

> **But if ye do not forgive, neither will your Father which is in heaven forgive your trespasses.**

Now look at Ephesians 4:30-32:

> **And grieve not the holy Spirit of God, whereby ye are sealed unto the day of redemption. Let all bitterness, and wrath, and anger, and clamour, and evil speaking, be put away from you, with all malice: And be ye kind one to another, tenderhearted, forgiving one another, even as God for Christ's sake hath forgiven you.**

Verse 30 says, "Grieve not the Holy Spirit of God." We already talked about the fact that one of the main things that grieves the Holy Ghost is an unforgiving spirit.

Verse 31 says, **Let all bitterness, and wrath, and anger, and clamour, and evil speaking, be put away from you, with all malice.** You see, when someone mistreats you, all this junk can come in if you're not careful. When someone wrongs you, you can become bitter. You can become angry. And you can want to get back at him or her.

When you are bitter and unforgiving, you are no good to yourself or your family. You will snap at them and tell them to shut up. How do I know that? Because we are all human, and we have to deal with these things in life. Every day isn't Sunday; in other words, we don't act perfectly and say, "Honey, I love you," all day every day. No, we're in human bodies. The soul and the body are not saved; they trick us and trip us up every now and then. Things come up, and there are problems we have to deal with. That's why we have God's Word; His Spirit; the gifts of the Spirit; the ministry gifts, such as pastors and teachers; and services where the Word is preached and taught—so we can "dump" the temptation to be unforgiving and receive a new load of grace and the Spirit!

## IF UNFORGIVENESS TRIPS YOU UP, REPENT AND GET BACK IN THE FAITH FIGHT!

I once dealt with a certain member of my church who had become tripped up by unforgiveness. As sweet as this woman is, she and one of her friends were not seeing things eye to eye. Her friend had not treated her properly in a certain situation. I came out into the church sanctuary one Sunday morning, and I could see by this church member's countenance that something was not right. Her spirit was grieved.

I went over to her to try to help her. I asked, "What's the matter?" She told me, and she admitted that she was being tripped up by what her friend had said to her. She was harboring unforgiveness in her heart. Then she prayed with me, and she became a new person! Before she prayed, I almost wanted to say in fun, "Will the real _____ please stand up!" But, afterward, her face was aglow once again with the joy of the Lord.

When you forgive someone for hurting you, it becomes to you as if that person never wronged you. When you forgive, you become a free man or woman. Your heart "condemneth you not" (1 John 3:20), and you have confidence toward God.

If the Spirit of God tells me I need to go to somebody and ask him or her to forgive me, God knows I will surely go. I'll go quickly. I'll *run* to that person. And when someone wrongs me, I will just as quickly forgive him or her. I refuse to hold a grudge or become bitter. I don't want to lose out on the blessings of God. I don't want to lose in my faith fights. I want to win against life's challenges. And I know the only way I'm going to be able to do that is to maintain an excellent spirit, even in the midst of temptations, tests and trials.

# Chapter 10

## *Count the Cost, Meet the Challenge and Obtain the Prize!*

We established in chapter 1 that the just shall live by faith and that to win in the challenges of life, you have to be prepared and willing to fight the good fight of faith. That's not bad news. That's *good* news, because the faith fight is a good fight. It's a fight that you *win*.

So we know that the just shall live by faith. The just shall live by *his* faith, not by anyone else's faith. And we know that faith should be a lifestyle. It is not the Father's will for you to live in defeat. It is not the Father's will for the enemy to beat you at every turn. It is not the Father's will for you to put off living in victory until you get to heaven. It is the Father's will that you live in victory *now*.

"That's great, Reverend Thompson. But how do I live in constant victory—every day—like the Father wants me to?" Remember I quoted First John 5:4, which says, **For whatsoever is born of God overcometh the world: and this is the victory that overcometh the world, even our faith.** The secret to your victory lies in your *faith.*

The Bible has a lot to say about this important subject of faith. Look at Jude 3:

> **Beloved, when I gave all diligence to write unto you of the common salvation, it was needful for me to write unto**

175

you, and exhort you that ye should earnestly contend for
the faith which was once delivered unto the saints.

That word "contend" means *to strive against rivals or difficulties;
to argue; to maintain or claim.* It also means *to uphold as true, right,
and proper.*[1] This verse is telling us to contend for the faith. That goes
right along with First Timothy 6:12, which says, **Fight the good fight
of faith, lay hold on eternal life, whereunto thou art also called, and
hast professed a good profession before many witnesses.**

God wants you to have a long, full, satisfied life with your needs
met in abundance. He wants you to have fullness of joy no matter
what the news media or the doctors say. But in order to give those
things to you, He has to have some cooperation from you. In other
words, God works with your *faith.* He has to see some faith to be able
to do in your life what He wants to do. Do you plan to go all the way
and obtain all that God has for you, whether it be spiritually, physically, mentally, emotionally or financially? If so, you're going to have
to do it by faith.

**But without faith it is impossible to please him: for he
that cometh to God must believe that he is, and that he is
a rewarder of them that diligently seek him.**

HEBREWS 11:6

Some people just want to use faith to get things. Certainly, you
have to use faith to receive the things that God has promised in His
Word. But faith is more than a tool; it is a lifestyle.

**And he that doubteth is damned if he eat, because he
eateth not of faith: for whatsoever is not of faith is sin.**

ROMANS 14:23

You are not going to get far in faith if you simply try faith but
then get off of your faith at the first gripe. The last part of Romans
14:23 says, **...whatsoever is not of faith is sin.** Since **whatsoever is**

176

**not of faith is sin**, then it stands to reason that we are to *live* by faith in every area of life.

I mean, really, you have to have faith as a Christian to so much as spit! You are supposed to live by faith. You are not supposed to use faith just to get what you want. You are to live by faith so when things come against you, you can hold steady in faith because you're living the lifestyle of faith.

Say this out loud: "My faith is pleasing to God, and where it is not pleasing to God, I am going to correct it. For it is impossible to please God without faith, and that which is not of faith is sin."

### COUNTING THE COST: CAN YOU REALLY HANDLE A LIFESTYLE OF FAITH AND VICTORY?

As you climb each rung on the ladder of faith, Satan will bring greater challenges to you. You see, a lifestyle of faith is a lifestyle of victory that brings glory to God, and Satan does not want God to get any glory. So if you can't stand the challenges, just stay on the rung where you are. Luke 14:28 talks about counting the cost. We do a lot of *talking* about living the life of faith, but when God wants us to do certain things, we have to be ready and willing to do them, and it will take faith. It will take standing against the threats and the challenges of the enemy. If you don't want to face that, then stay on the rung where you are. Let somebody else move up to the next rung.

Some Christians will never make it, because they are too "nice" to stand in the face of a challenge and continue to fight the good fight of faith. In other words, if someone criticized them, they'd back off, saying, "Oh, okay. If you don't like it, I'll stop doing it." They are too concerned with being crowd-pleasers. If someone criticized their nice shoes, they'd stop wearing them and go get a *not*-so-nice pair of shoes.

But if God is prospering you in your obedient life of faith, there are just some material blessings that are going to overtake you. Certain things are going to come along and be added to you. If you keep digging into God's Word and working for God and loving Him, there are certain amenities that you can't stop God from giving you.

I tell you, I'm not playing around with faith. I have set my rudders. I am going to live the life of faith, and I am not going to back up for anybody. I am not backing up for your grandma or mine either! I'm going all the way with this life of faith. The faith life is a *real* life.

MEET THE CHALLENGE AND PLEASE THE FATHER

Certainly, people are going to come against you, but you have to stay with faith, no matter what comes!

**But with many of them** [the children of Israel] **God was not well pleased: for they were overthrown in the wilderness.**

1 CORINTHIANS 10:5

We need to find out what displeased the Father here, because what displeased the Father then displeases Him now. The last part of this verse tells us what displeased Him: ...**for they were overthrown in the wilderness.** In other words, God was not pleased with them, because they did not live in victory. He was not pleased, because they had all they needed to cause them *not* to be overthrown, yet they were still overthrown.

It's the same way today. When God has given you everything you need to win, yet you are losing, He is not pleased. Now, I have to qualify "losing." Losing is living by your feelings and letting go of your faith when things get tough. If you are genuinely walking by faith and in the light of God's Word, you may appear in your circumstances to be losing. Your faith may not appear to be working. But it is working! No matter what it looks like, you are not losing; you are

178

*winning!* You are gaining! You see, with faith in God, you can't lose! In God's eyes, appearances and circumstances do not have anything to do with winning or losing. God is a circumstance changer!

### WALKING BY FEELINGS INSTEAD OF BY FAITH WILL DEFEAT YOU

You can't live by your feelings and walk with God in a way that is pleasing to Him. Why? Because feelings are flaky; they are always changing. For example, you don't feel great every day. You don't feel like praising God every day. But you need to praise Him anyway, when you feel like it and when you don't.

Have you ever tried to walk with God by your feelings? One day you're up, and the next day you're down. It is impossible to be sturdy, steady and strong in faith and walk by feelings at the same time. It takes effort to walk and stand by faith. It takes teaching, training and constantly submitting yourself to the authority of God's Word.

First Corinthians 10:5 is the companion verse to Hebrews 11:6, which says, **But without faith it is impossible to please him....** First Corinthians 10:5 will put a "whipping" on you if you are not serious about living a life of faith.

Now, why wasn't God pleased? God was not pleased, because they were overthrown. Can you see that? They had all that they needed to *not* be overthrown, and when they were overthrown despite all that power and the promise of God, it displeased the Father. And in your own life, in the areas where you are failing because your faith is slack—because you haven't put into practice what God has told you— He is not pleased with you.

There are areas in which some people are letting Satan run over them and take authority over *them* when *they* should be taking authority over *him*. And they know better. The Father is not pleased.

⸺∞⸻ You Need Not Be Overthrown by Challenges ⸻∞⸺

Read that verse again: **But with many of them God was not well pleased: for they were overthrown in the wilderness.** They should not have been overthrown. Why? Because they were in covenant with God. And those who are living the life of faith should not be overthrown either, because they are in covenant with God too. He is their protector and provider.

Now, notice something in Hebrews 3 in connection with the Israelites' displeasing the Father.

> **Harden not your hearts, as in the provocation, in the day of temptation in the wilderness: When your fathers tempted me, proved me, and saw my works forty years. Wherefore I was grieved with that generation, and said, They do alway err in their heart; and they have not known my ways.**
>
> HEBREWS 3:8-10

Look at the first part of verse 10: **Wherefore I was grieved with that generation....** It brings grievance to God when we who live by faith allow challenges to stop us. He is not pleased when we are overthrown. Why? He wants us to get up and fight the good fight of faith. He wants us to close our mouths when they need to be closed and open them when they need to be opened. In other words, in the midst of a challenge, if you don't know what to say, don't say anything. Don't cop out and go talk to somebody else about all of your problems to try to get him or her to sympathize with you and pat you on the back.

What good is it to get someone to pat you on your back if the devil's *riding* your back already? What good is it for someone to say, "It is going to be all right after awhile"? What good is that? The Lord has already told you in His Word that it's going to be all right if you are really trusting Him.

Challenges are temporary. As long as you're living for God and doing what's right according to His Word, anything that comes against you is only temporary. The challenge can't last. There is nothing greater than God. Is anything too hard for Him? You are in God's corner—and you think you are going to go to the center of the ring and lose the fight? What kind of messed up thinking is that? God *can't* lose.

Genesis 37 begins the account of someone who had the opportunity to allow the delay of his God-given dream to overthrow him. His name was Joseph, and he went from the *pit* to the *palace* to the *prison* and, finally, to *Pharaoh*—to the throne of Pharaoh to be his right-hand man! (See Genesis 37-50.)

Joseph's brothers hated him because he was operating in a different realm than the one they were operating in. He was walking with God, having spiritual insight, and his brothers did not like that. They began to hate him and were envious of him because of his dream that he would rise to greatness (Genesis 37:5-11).

## ARE YOU A DREAMER OR A DRIFTER?

You see, when you are a dreamer for God, some people will hate you. Your becoming a dreamer will expose the indifference of someone who isn't a dreamer. But if you become stale and stagnant spiritually, never progressing and prospering, then you will blend into the crowd.

Dreamers become a threat to drifters, to common folks who don't want to do or be anything for God. Joseph became a threat to his brothers. They said, "We've got to stop this dreamer." And, today, drifters will say about a dreamer, "We've got to stop this person who says the Word works."

Joseph's brothers devised a way to try to stop him. They made a mockery of his dream. They made it out to be a lie. But hell will freeze over before the Word of God becomes a lie! You simply can't make the Word out to be a lie. If you disagree with the Word, that Word is going to make you out to be the liar every time.

Don't be afraid when your faith is challenged. When others lie about you and start rumors against you and falsely accuse you, you've got to stand your ground in faith. Many of the Old Testament saints did better at this than most of us do today. We live in a "push-button" society. We have drive-throughs, microwaves, remote controls, instant this and instant that. And we let that carry over into our spiritual lives. That microwave mentality flows over into our spirits, and we want to have microwave faith!

But it doesn't work that way. We have to fight the good fight of faith and keep on fighting until we win. Instead, if we don't have our answer "warmed up" and ready in thirty seconds—in microwave timing—we are dissatisfied! But sometimes answers take longer. Sometimes they take thirty *days*. But I tell you, a situation shouldn't drag on and on if you are putting the force of the Word on it. If it does drag on and on, your faith is not working properly.

## INTEGRITY, DEDICATION AND COMMITMENT WILL KEEP YOU AND PUT YOU OVER IN LIFE'S FIGHTS

There are some things in connection with faith that we need to put into practice if we want our faith to be effective. One of those things is *integrity*. Can you recognize integrity when you see it? Do you see it in your life? If you don't, then you don't have it, and you need to work on it. If you are going to answer your faith challenges in life, you must know something about integrity.

Another characteristic that works in connection with your faith is dedication and commitment. You have to be dedicated and committed to the Word of God and to the plan of God for your life, or you won't stick with it when your faith is challenged. Integrity, dedication and commitment are recognizable characteristics that go along with the faith life.

We see an example of these characteristics in three Hebrew men—Shadrach, Meshach and Abednego. These boys wanted to live in victory and possess all that God had for them. They wanted to live in the fullness of their potential in God and to experience more of God's kind of life. They became a threat to some people, so they were threatened in return.

Let me give you a little background concerning what happened.

**Nebuchadnezzar the king made an image of gold, whose height was threescore cubits, and the breadth thereof six cubits: he set it up in the plain of Dura, in the province of Babylon.**

**Then an herald cried aloud, To you it is commanded, O people, nations, and languages, That at what time ye hear the sound of the cornet, flute, harp, sackbut, psaltery, dulcimer, and all kinds of musick, ye fall down and worship the golden image that Nebuchadnezzar the king hath set up: And whoso falleth not down and worshippeth shall the same hour be cast into the midst of a burning fiery furnace. Therefore at that time, when all the people heard the sound of the cornet, flute, harp, sackbut, psaltery, and all kinds of musick, all the people, the nations, and the languages, fell down and worshipped the golden image that Nebuchadnezzar the king had set up.**

DANIEL 3:1,4-7

The king had set up a golden image. He had all his musicians come out, and when they started playing, everyone in the kingdom had to bow down and worship that image.

183

Now, there were three boys whose faith was being challenged, and they would not bow or concede. They stood their ground and fought the good fight of faith.

**Wherefore at that time certain Chaldeans came near, and accused the Jews [saying]...**

**There are certain Jews whom thou hast set over the affairs of the province of Babylon, Shadrach, Meshach, and Abednego; these men, O king, have not regarded thee: they serve not thy gods, nor worship the golden image which thou hast set up. Then Nebuchadnezzar in his rage and fury commanded to bring Shadrach, Meshach, and Abednego. Then they brought these men before the king. Nebuchadnezzar spake and said unto them, Is it true, O Shadrach, Meshach, and Abednego, do not ye serve my gods, nor worship the golden image which I have set up? Now if ye be ready that at what time ye hear the sound of the cornet, flute, harp, sackbut, psaltery, and dulcimer, and all kinds of musick, ye fall down and worship the image which I have made; well: but if ye worship not, ye shall be cast the same hour into the midst of a burning fiery furnace; and who is that God that shall deliver you out of my hands?**

DANIEL 3:8,12-15

After the Chaldeans accused the three Hebrew boys, the king had a personal interview with them. Notice they were accused. Those Chaldeans didn't like Shadrach, Meshach and Abednego, and they wanted to see them suffer. And, today, there will be those who will accuse you, too, if you are walking by faith.

When the king sent for the three Hebrews, he said to them, "When the music starts playing, I want all of you to bow. And if you don't, I am going to cast you into the fiery furnace." You see, that was the challenge. Their faith was being challenged.

Then King Nebuchadnezzar said, **And who is that God that shall deliver you out of my hands?** (v. 15).

Notice that Shadrach, Meshach and Abednego were in one accord when they answered the king.

> **Shadrach, Meshach, and Abednego, answered and said to the king, O Nebuchadnezzar, we are not careful to answer thee in this matter. If it be so, our God whom we serve is able to deliver us from the burning fiery furnace, and he will deliver us out of thine hand, O king. But if not, be it known unto thee, O king, that we will not serve thy gods, nor worship the golden image which thou hast set up.**
>
> DANIEL 3:16-18

They answered and said unto the king, **We are not careful to answer thee in this matter.** A footnote in my Bible says, "We *have no need* to answer thee...." In other words, they were saying, "We're not even thinking about your threat."

You know, instead of talking and worrying about some of the things that come against you in life, you should just say, "I'm not even going to think about this." You should go on.

Notice what happened next. The three Hebrews said, **If it be so, our God whom we serve is able to deliver us from the burning fiery furnace, and he will deliver us out of thine hand, O king** (v. 17). In other words, they were saying, "If it happens that it's true that you're going to do what you say you're going to do, our God whom we serve is able to deliver us from the burning, fiery furnace. And He will deliver us."

—∞— LET YOUR FAITH DO THE TALKING —∞—

*That is faith talking!* Now, those boys were facing a fiery furnace, and they were not even born again. Could you say that their faith was

185

being challenged? Yet, today, many Christians will have some little thing go wrong and will be thrown completely off course! Those three Hebrews were talking to the king! Some people let some bigmouth get them all upset and off course in their faith fight!

Now, I want you to understand something about the first three words of verse 18. In verse 17, Shadrach, Meshach and Abednego had said, **If it be so, our God whom we serve is able to deliver us from the burning fiery furnace, and he will deliver us out of thine hand, O king.**

Then notice the next three words they spoke: BUT IF NOT, **be it known unto thee, O king, that we will not serve thy gods, nor worship the golden image which thou hast set up.**

You see, they were not saying, "But if the Lord does not deliver us, we will not serve your gods." No, they were saying, "But if you *don't* throw us into the fiery furnace, we're *still* not going to worship your gods."

—∞— GOD IS ABLE AND WILLING TO DELIVER YOU! —∞—

Shadrach, Meshach and Abednego had said, "We are not careful to answer thee in this matter" (v. 16). Do you know what the "matter" was? The matter was that they were not going to bow down to any god but the true God! Listen to what they said: "If it be so that you throw us into the fire, our God is able to deliver us. We know that. And not only is He able, but He *will* deliver us out of your hand."

Now, notice in their example the one thing missing from their faith confession. I talked about it briefly in a previous chapter, but it is an important ingredient to fighting the good fight of faith and overcoming the challenges to your faith. The three Hebrews said they knew God was *able* to deliver them. And they knew He *would* deliver them. But notice they did not know *how* God was going to do it! Do

186

you know why? Because the "how" did not belong to them. The knowledge that God was able and willing belonged to them, but the "how" belonged to God!

When you are operating in faith, it is your job to come to the point of knowing that God is able. It is your job to come to the point of knowing that He is willing. But the "how" and the "when" are up to God. We get on God's territory when we try to mentally reason how God is going to come through for us. Our job is just to study the Scripture and to thoroughly have faith and confidence in His willingness and His ability to bless us.

That is where we get messed up. We want to know the "how." But once you know the "how," you are no longer in faith. If you know *how,* you are in the flesh. If you always knew the next step, you wouldn't need God. So leave the "how" up to God. Concentrate on His ability and His willingness to deliver you, and God will take care of the "how."

We need to learn to be like the three Hebrew boys. They refused to bow to the golden image and instead made a bold declaration of faith. In much the same way, we need to refuse to bow to the god of persecutions, lies and accusations. We need to just continue serving the God of truth, love and victory.

## The Word Will Prepare You for Challenges That Are Full of Fury

Let me tell you something else about faith's challenges. Sometimes they can be full of fury! They can come at you strong and hard. Let's continue reading in Daniel 3.

> **Then was Nebuchadnezzar full of fury, and the form of his visage was changed against Shadrach, Meshach, and Abednego: therefore he spake, and commanded that they**

187

should heat the furnace one seven times more than it was wont to be heated.

DANIEL 3:19

Have you ever noticed that some people can talk so mean to you, it's like fire is coming out of their mouths? They want to get at you so badly! In verse 19, it says, **Then was Nebuchadnezzar full of fury, and the form of his visage was changed against Shadrach, Meshach, and Abednego....** Nebuchadnezzar became so angry that he commanded the furnace to be heated seven times hotter than normal!

There are going to be challenges in your life, and some are going to be full of fury. So learn to walk by faith and to fight the faith fight when you're faced with those challenges. Don't always be calling everybody you know and depending on the faith of others to get you through. Sometimes people will misguide you. They may just be trying to help, but they end up putting more wood on the fire of your fiery test! So learn to depend on God, not man.

**And he [Nebuchadnezzar] commanded the most mighty men that were in his army to bind Shadrach, Meshach, and Abednego, and to cast them into the burning fiery furnace. Then these men were bound in their coats, their hosen, and their hats, and their other garments, and were cast into the midst of the burning fiery furnace.**

DANIEL 3:20,21

The three Hebrews were bound in their coats, socks, hats and other garments and were actually cast into the midst of the fiery furnace. Sometimes before God can deliver us, we have to go into the "furnace"!

Someone might say, "But I don't want any furnace experience. I want the air conditioner!" But when your faith gets to a certain level, you can't get to the next level without a greater challenge. It is just like a man picking up weights. If he's been picking up eighty pounds

188

for two years, it is time to change the rack. He's not developing that much more muscle. He needs to go up to the 120-pound weights.

It's the same way with faith. You've got to stretch your faith to cover greater challenges. If you are just lying around doing the same things with your faith that you have already been doing, you won't grow in faith.

## GOD WILL NEVER LEAVE YOU

I want to show you some more faith truths from the account of the Hebrew boys in the fiery furnace.

> **Therefore because the king's commandment was urgent, and the furnace exceeding hot, the flame of the fire slew those men that took up Shadrach, Meshach, and Abednego. And these three men, Shadrach, Meshach, and Abednego, fell down bound into the midst of the burning fiery furnace.**
>
> DANIEL 3:22,23

Now, it seems in these verses that God was not delivering them. Where was God? Have you ever asked that question? (If not, have you ever *wanted* to ask that question?) I mean, after you quote all those Scriptures and push all the right buttons, so to speak, and yet it looks like nothing is happening, your flesh wants to say, "Where is your God now?"

He is still there! He is there, and if you will remain full of faith and refuse to bow, there will come a time when God will say, "That's enough."

The Father sees you standing. He looks at Jesus, Jesus looks at Him and the Holy Spirit brings a report too. They have a meeting in heaven, and the Father says, "Now that is enough. I am going to go take care of it now. That is enough training for today."

With the Father, Jesus and the Holy Spirit on your side, you know you can't lose! No weapon formed against you shall prosper (Isaiah 54:17)! When the enemy comes in like a flood, the Spirit shall lift up a standard against him (Isaiah 59:19). Hallelujah!

That's exactly what happened for the three Hebrews in the fiery furnace.

> Then Nebuchadnezzar the king was astonied, and rose up in haste, and spake, and said unto his counsellors, Did not we cast three men bound into the midst of the fire? They answered and said unto the king, True, O king. He answered and said, Lo, I see four men loose, walking in the midst of the fire, and they have no hurt; and the form of the fourth is like the Son of God.
>
> DANIEL 3:24,25

The king's men had thrown three men into that furnace; but when the king looked in, he saw four; and the form of the fourth man in that fire was like the Son of God!

## WHEN YOU SUCCESSFULLY MEET THE CHALLENGE, GOD WILL REWARD YOU

You see, when you stand up to the challenge, even your enemies will have to pay attention and confess that they were wrong.

> Then Nebuchadnezzar came near to the mouth of the burning fiery furnace, and spake, and said, Shadrach, Meshach, and Abednego, ye servants of the most high God, come forth, and come hither. Then Shadrach, Meshach, and Abednego, came forth of the midst of the fire. And the princes, governors, and captains, and the king's counsellors, being gathered together, saw these men, upon whose bodies the fire had no power, nor was an hair of their head

singed, neither were their coats changed, nor the smell of fire had passed on them. **Then Nebuchadnezzar spake, and said, Blessed be the God of Shadrach, Meshach, and Abednego, who hath sent his angel, and delivered his servants that trusted in him, and have changed the king's word, and yielded their bodies, that they might not serve nor worship any god, except their own God. Therefore I make a decree, That every people, nation, and language, which speak any thing amiss against the God of Shadrach, Meshach, and Abednego, shall be cut in pieces, and their houses shall be made a dunghill: because there is no other God that can deliver after this sort. Then the king promoted Shadrach, Meshach, and Abednego, in the province of Babylon.**

DANIEL 3:26-30

King Nebuchadnezzar saw the deliverance that God wrought on behalf of those three boys, and he admitted that God was indeed God! The king said, **Blessed be the God of Shadrach, Meshach, and Abednego, who hath sent his angel, and delivered his servants that trusted in him, and have changed the king's word, and yielded their bodies, that they might not serve nor worship any god, except their own God** (v. 28).

Verse 30 says, **Then the king promoted Shadrach, Meshach, and Abednego, in the province of Babylon.**

The king promoted Shadrach, Meshach and Abednego in his kingdom. But, actually, promotion comes from God. It comes from meeting the challenges of life instead of being overthrown by them. It comes when you are faithful to God and His Word. He will promote you if you count the cost when your faith is challenged and if you meet that challenge head-on, fighting the good fight of faith.

191

Fighting the good fight of faith is a winning battle! You can't lose! You may experience temporary delays, but you can't lose if you just stick with it. God will always bring you out. God *will* deliver you!

# Endnotes

## Chapter 1
[1] Webster, "profess," p. 939.

[2] Random House, "hold," p. 910.

## Chapter 2
[1] Webster, "envy," p. 417.

## Chapter 3
[1] Webster, "certify," p. 223.

## Chapter 7
[1] Random House, "sift," p. 1778.

## Chapter 10
[1] Random House, "contend," pp. 438-439.

# References

*Random House Compact Unabridged Dictionary, Special Second Edition.* New York: Random House, Inc., 1996.

*Webster Ninth New Collegiate Dictionary.* Springfield, MA: Merriam-Webster, Inc., 1986.

# About The Author

**Dr. Leroy Thompson Sr.** is the pastor and founder of Word of Life Christian Center in Darrow, Louisiana, a growing and thriving body of believers from various walks of life. He has been in the ministry for twenty-two years, serving for twenty years as a pastor. Even though he completed his undergraduate degree and theology doctorate and was an instructor for several years at a Christian Bible college in Louisiana, it wasn't until 1983, when he received the baptism in the Holy Spirit, that the revelation knowledge of God's Word changed his life; and it continues to increase his ministry. Dr. Thompson attributes the success of his life and ministry to his reliance on the Word of God and to being filled with the Holy Spirit and led by the Spirit of God. Today Dr. Thompson travels across the United States taking the message of ministerial excellence, dedication and discipline to the Body of Christ.

To contact Dr. Leroy Thompson Sr.,
write:


Dr. Leroy Thompson Sr.
Ever Increasing Word Ministries
P.O. Box 7
Darrow, Louisiana 70725


*Please include your prayer requests
and comments when you write.*

# Other Books by Dr. Leroy Thompson Sr.

*Money Cometh!*

*The Voice of Jesus:*
*Speaking God's Word With Authority*

Available from your local bookstore

**HARRISON HOUSE**
Tulsa, Oklahoma 74153

## The Harrison House Vision

Proclaiming the truth and the power
Of the Gospel of Jesus Christ
With excellence;

Challenging Christians to
Live victoriously,
Grow spiritually,
Know God intimately.